The Abandoned Farmers

The Abandoned Farmers

His Humorous Account of a Retreat
from the City to the Farm

Irvin S. Cobb

Introduction by Hannah M. Biggs

Hastings College Press | Hastings, Nebraska

Introduction © 2016 by Hastings College Press

Text © 1916, 1919 by The Curtis Publishing Company. © 1920 by George H. Doran Company. This book has fallen into the public domain and is no longer subject to copyright protection.

All rights reserved. No part of this book may be used or reproduced in any manner whatsoever without permission from the publisher, except in the case of brief quotations embodied in critical articles and reviews.

Production Staff
Dakota Anderson
Emilie Barnes
Kaitlyn Baucom
Allie Belitz
Hannah Currey
Razvan Dobrin
Kaitlin Grode
Rachel Jesske
Alex Kreikemeier
Brooke MacLeod
Holly Wolfe

ISBN-10: 1-952885-41-5
ISBN-13: 978-1-942885-41-2

Note on the text: This edition has been reset from the 1920 edition. Original spelling and grammatical conventions have been maintained, except in the case of publishing errors in the 1920 edition. The original punctuation has been maintained but updated using modern conventions (e.g., eliminating spaces around dashes).

Manufactured in the United States of America

Contents

Which Really Is an Introduction in Disguise.......... vii

I	Which Really Is a Preface in Disguise....... 1
II	The Start of a Dream................... 5
III	Three Years Elapse.................... 37
IV	Happy Days for Major Gloom.......... 59
V	In Which We Bore for Water........... 73
VI	Two More Years Elapse................. 91
VII	"And Sold To—".................... 117
VIII	The Adventure of Lady Maude......... 151
IX	Us Landed Proprietors............... 165

Which Really Is an Introduction in Disguise

Hannah M. Biggs

Irvin S. Cobb writes in his original preface to *The Abandoned Farmers*, "It is really the inclination of the average reader to skip prefaces. For this I do not in the least blame him. Skipping the preface is one of my favorite literary pursuits. To catch me napping a preface must creep up quietly and take me, as it were, unawares" (1).

Now as I see it you, the reader, have three choices. You too may skip the introduction to this book. Perhaps Cobb himself would have been pleased with your choice. You may skim the introduction simply on the off chance you find it helpful, elucidative, and informative. Or, you can read this introduction with wholehearted curiosity, engagement, and interest. I, of course, would prefer you choose the latter of the three. Cobb himself masqueraded his own preface to *The Abandoned Farmers* as a first chapter entitled, "Which is Really a Preface in Disguise" to, as he said, "hoodwink" his readers into reading the preface (2). Perhaps this newest edition will succeed in doing just the same.

The Legend

Irvin Shrewsbury Cobb (1876–1944) is now perhaps best known as the namesake of a historic bridge over the Ohio River, more often called the Brookport Bridge (Holth et al.); a former large-event hotel recently turned into a low-income apartment complex in Paducah, Kentucky ("Hotel Irvin Cobb"); a campsite in Murray, Kentucky (Dietrich and Dietrich); and/or the namesake for Yorkana Company's prime line of 1920s cigars ("Irvin S. Cobb Inner Cigar"). Sadly, the intricacies of Cobb's legacy, life, and times have, except in rare academic circles, been lost. Once "the subject of daily discussions in the barber shops of America" in the 1920s and '30s, Cobb's popularity has dwindled and, along with it, his important "legacy to American humor" (Chatterton i).

 Cobb, who, "in appearance [was] rather bulky, standing at six feet high, not especially beautiful, a light roan in color, with a black mane and a ... figure ... [that] might be called bunchy in places" (T.W.), began his career at age sixteen when he quit school and began writing for his hometown newspaper, the *Paducah Daily News* (which he became editor of at the age of nineteen) (Drew 78). Later Cobb worked briefly for the *Louisville Evening Post* before moving to New York in 1904 to start work at the *Evening Sun*. While there, he was charged with covering the Russian-Japanese Peace conference in New Hampshire, a meeting that led to the Treaty of Portsmouth, which effectively ended the Russo-Japanese War (1904–5). His coverage portrayed the various personalities involved in the peace treaty efforts, including that of intrepid U.S. President Theodore Roosevelt (who later won a Nobel Peace Prize for his instrumental role in the negotiations). Cobb brought that story to life, painting lucid portrayals of all the attendees' unique personalities and foibles, and the *Evening Sun* ran his piece under the title, "Making Peace at Portsmouth." It was this story that caught the eye of Joseph Pulitzer, editor of *New York World*, who later offered Cobb a job on his staff. Cobb took the job, and he became the highest-paid staff reporter in the United States at that time (Hoover 4). In 1911, Cobb joined the staff of the *The Saturday Evening Post*. Later dubbed a "national institution" because of his work as a World War I combat reporter for the *Post*, Cobb's first-hand accounts of combat in Europe were one of the first of their kind, and they earned him an abnormally large readership for that time, an estimated audience of more than two million readers (Grinnell 252). In 1924, Cobb was lured by the "deep pockets" of *Cosmopolitan*'s editor, Ray Long, and publisher, William Randolph Hearst (Drew 79).

 At the time of his appointment under the auspices of Hearst, Cobb was already a prolific author of nonfiction, fiction, and short stories alike, and he moved in some of the greatest literary circles of his time, calling the likes of O. Henry, Theodore Dreiser, Rudyard Kipling, Sinclair Lewis, and Eugene O'Neill acquaintances and friends. His best known works were the "Old Judge Priest" stories about a Paducah lawyer named Judge Priest. These stories were later collected in the book *Old Judge Priest* (1915). Much of Cobb's most popular work (and for which he became well-known) was released serially in magazines like *The Saturday Evening Post*, a magazine full of stories "to be passed around, waved in the air, or stabbed by a forefinger, depending what the speaker thought of the author at the moment" (Chatterton i).

Throughout his life, Cobb worked as a newspaper journalist, magazine columnist, reporter, and author, but he also worked as a screenwriter and actor. He licensed his short stories for silent-film adaptations, and he acted as the star player of one of the earliest experimental sound shorts, *Irvin S. Cobb, All-American Storyteller*, in 1921. He wrote titles for two more well-known silent films, *Peck's Bad Boy* and *Pardon My French* (both 1921), among others (Eder). Cobb's writing remained popular into the early 1930s and served as source material for many big Hollywood films, including *The Woman Accused* (1933), starring Hollywood legend Cary Grant. His "Old Judge Priest" stories were turned into movies as well. John Ford directed two movies based on these stories, *Judge Priest* in 1934 with Will Rogers in the star role and *The Sun Shines Bright* in 1953. But Cobb's Hollywood roles did not stop there. He went on to act in ten movies between 1932 and 1938, starting his acting career in the 1910s in John W. Noble's *Our Mutual Girl* (1914) and in Cecille B. DeMille's *The Arab* (1915) (Drew 79). He later played bigger roles in *Pepper* and *Everybody's Old Man* (both 1936), as well as *Hawaii Calls* (1938) ("Irvin S. Cobb"). Cobb was so well-known among the rich and glamourous of The Golden Age of Hollywood that he hosted the 7th Academy Awards.

A Rural Southern Legacy

Some of the humor in *The Abandoned Farmers* relies on readers' knowledge of Cobb's public persona—surely such a witty and urbane man would be a disaster as a farmer! But farm life was not so alien to Cobb. His boyhood was spent on a small farm within the city limits of Paducah, Kentucky, which is nestled due south of the Ohio River. He lived with his grandparents, parents, a brother, two sisters, an African American cook and housekeeper, and Uncle Rufus—an African American everyman's man who had his own residence at the back of the property (Hoover 4). The small, two-acre farm consisted of a ten-room house, cow shed, smokehouse, stable with an ample hayloft, orchard, and a dilapidated outhouse jokingly referred to by the family as "Miss Jones" (Cobb, "Exit" 46). Mr. Cobb fondly recounted his early years spent on the farm in his autobiography, *Exit Laughing* (1941). Of those farm-spent years, Cobb declared,

> Nowhere on the American map, I insist, could there have
> been a playground more admirably devised to fulfill the
> cravings of healthy, adventure-seeking youngsters....
> fruit trees to be pillaged and climbed; tangles of unshorn
> shrubbery; a grape arbor and a tool hutch ... Then also
> the smokehouse, its sooty rafters jeweled with fat hams
> like eardrops and pendent strips of cured middling meat
> and necklaces of homemade sausages; the well house, with
> its crocks and pans and jugs and buckets submerged in
> bricked shallow tanks and it such a lovely retreat for sultry
> days; a densely populated chicken yard; lofty manure piles
> in the horse lot and beneath the corner eaves, where the
> tin gutter sprouts come down from the roof, open barrels
> to catch rain water and incidentally to provide breeding
> places for millions of wiggle-tailed larvae. ("Exit" 46–47)

His decision to buy and renovate a farm in rural New York state should not be a surprise, then. In keeping with his agrarian Kentucky heritage and the fashion of his adult years in the late 1910s to own a farm, Cobb would not live long away from the countryside, away from a landscape that had clearly provided him hours of pleasurable entertainment and adventure in his youth.

Cobb's early Kentucky experiences actually helped to create his popularity, especially in the "Old Judge Priest" stories. Although they were well-received when released serially in the *The Saturday Evening Post* and later collected for the aforementioned book, these stories do not stand up well today. Laced with racist slurs and stereotypically portrayed African American characters, the stories are deemed, as James W. Grinnell aptly calls them, an "outright embarrassment" by today's standards (251). Grinnell's summation is quite correct, for Cobb's stories depicted stereotypical caricatures of African Americans and their speech patterns, including common minstrel dialect: "dem" and "dose" and "I's gwine." The cartoons in his recipe book, *Irvin S. Cobb's Own Recipe Book* (1934) (which, as it happens, is mostly dedicated to cocktails) also controversially depict pictures of African American servants tending to the Southern gentry (Rodell). Cobb even said, when asked to compile a list of imaginary, fictional dinner guests, "As a Southerner, I'd want Uncle Remus. Naturally we might not want him as a guest since we still draw the color line in some respects. But at least he could wait on the table. He'd give a real American tone to the proceedings by reason of the fact that he is an authentic, black-skinned American and so utterly different from the average popular conception today of what a real negro is" ("Fiction Characters" 15).

Cobb's stories of the south are what you might expect from a white author born in Kentucky, a former Confederate state, in the year Reconstruction came to an end. His earliest years were marked by an era of Jim Crow laws and other forms of racial segregation, and his stories depicted a sentimentalized fantasy of the South already fading fast from view. His was a region with a cast of, as Bruce Eder describes it, "loveable eccentrics, colorful reprobates, upright and honorable civic leaders, and—most controversially, in retrospect—contented and deferential African Americans" (Eder).

Film adaptations of Cobb's stories, much like their own source material, were also tinged with racist, Jim Crow–era language and undertones. Public opinion of Cobb's writing declined rapidly in his later years, and much of this had to do with director John Ford's adaptations of his "Old Judge Priest" stories into two different films, *Judge Priest* (1934) and *The Sun Shines Bright* (which premiered in 1953, almost a decade after Cobb's death). In fact, Ford's decision to accurately portray the "Old Judge Priest" stories, including a lynching scene in *The Sun Shines Bright* and the stereotypical portrayal of an African American character, Jeff Poindexter, were viewed as controversial by many circles for their tasteless, insensitive portrayal of African Americans. By the 1950s, "many of the values embraced in the characters and stories [of Cobb's] were being knocked head over heels by new legislation and Supreme Court decisions," especially since *The Sun Shines Bright* premiered one year before the tantamount Brown v. Board of Education Supreme Court ruling (Drew 79). However, despite his later fall from grace and fame, Cobb was a beloved man of his time with resounding influence on both print and screen of the 1920s and '30s. And not all of the texts he produced during this prolific career are tinged with the racism of his southern stories. Many of his lesser-known texts, especially his purely humorous ones—like *The Abandoned Farmers*—have since suffered because of the critical tailspin of Cobb's career.

The Abandoned Farmers

The Abandoned Farmers, sometimes known by its full title, *The Abandoned Farmers: His Humorous Account of a Retreat from the City to the Country*, is pure farce. Humorous, engaging, and rapid-paced, this tale is downright funny. The story is told from a first person point of view, and Cobb attempts to elucidate for his readers the finer, yet all the more gruelling, aspects of buying a so-called abandoned (i.e., run-down, deserted) farm and making it one's own family homestead. Trials and tribulations abound, and Cobb's perception and description of it all make for a quick, enjoyable read. And, most fortunately, unlike some of Cobb's other work, *The Abandoned Farmers* suffers no distasteful racial slurs nor bleak characterizations. Instead, the story is bright, forthcoming, and engaging.

Cobb's text is a work of nonfiction, a story that has "a basis of verity, as all things in this life properly should have ... but ... largely it deals with what more or less is figurative and fanciful" (*Abandoned* 2). Cobb assures his readers of the truthfulness of his claims throughout *The Abandoned Farmers* when he points out the lies he has, supposedly, placed in the text: these "figment[s] of the imagination," such as the missing will found in the ruins of an old mill and the detailed passage recounting the search for a lost heir (*Abandoned* 2). Cobb tells us these two "figments of the imagination" can be found on page fifty-five—a page number that reveals nothing but a blank page in the original Doran Company edition! A blank page! We readers are left with no lines, no lies, on a blank page. We were tricked. Cobb must have been laughing at us. So, the readers must assume then that all Cobb tells us is truth, for even his lies were not printed. Required of us readers therefore is an implicit trust in our narrator, Cobb himself.

Cobb and his family did indeed move out to the countryside to one of these so-called abandoned farms. The Cobbs purchased sixty acres of land in 1916 in the northern part of Westchester County near Ossining, New York. The land itself was once the site of a grand estate complete with a farmer's cottage, a frame house, cow barn, coach house, ice house, and other smaller buildings. Most of these buildings, as *The Abandoned Farmers* recounts, were in states of incredible disrepair, and only the barn could be salvaged as a sort of temporary residence for the family until their country home was built. Although they could not move into their dream country home until some time after 1920, after *The Abandoned Farmers* had been published in its nine-chapter finished version, they moved into the converted barn and dubbed their new estate, Rebel Ridge.

The Cobbs were not unique in their choice to move to the country. Right during America's nationwide 'back-to-the-land'

An Introduction in Disguise   xiii

movement, when there rang out "the first great outcry ... regarding abandoned farms, [and] a companion chorus was raised about the back-to-the-land movement," Cobb joined the throngs of Americans moving into these "ready-made farms" (Laut 3). Even before Ralph Borsodi's *Flight from the City* of 1933 jolted the nation's city dwellers out of their urban (and urbane) sprawl, country magazines and city newspapers were urging people to move to the countryside to take up the vast acres of abandoned, east coast farmland. All the rage at the time, too, were these so-called abandoned farms, and many well-to-do city folks of the east coast were moving to the countryside to find these plots to take them up, remodel them to their more posh likings, and settle down with their families away from the hustle and bustle of the "feverish metropolitan influences, which radiating from the city ... [where] twice a day, or oftener ... [you are] packed in with countless fellow tired business men in the tired cars of the tired Subway" (Cobb, *Abandoned* 23, 39). One writer for the *Oakland Tribune* writes in 1920,

> A few years ago the abandoned farm first rose over the horizon like an easy dream of promise if any such performance, even in metaphor, is possible. The public ... was offered magazine articles telling them all about all of the Connecticut farmers who turned their plowshares into fountain pens and who turned their backs on their homesteads and went into the town. The farms were left to care for themselves and it was intimated that anyone who happened along could have them for a song. ("The Abandoned Farmers")

Numerous agricultural history books detail the plight of the abandoned farm, especially of the east coast farm, a region where "the abandoned farm was not the real agricultural problem, but only a by-product of an agricultural disaster that had come to New England with the development of the West and the building of the railroads to the seaboard" (Bercaw and Hannay 648). But when reports came of nearly 400,000 east coast families leaving behind almost ten million acres of farms, "that is, an area of 16,000 square miles, equal to thirteen times the size of Rhode Island, or three times that of Connecticut, or twice that of Massachusettes or New Jersey," the hunt for abandoned farms was on (Laut 3). The wealthy descended onto the open vastness like a willing flock of docile sheep.

The Cobbs chose a beautiful plot of land close to friends who had also moved out to the country, and it was not long before even more friends followed suit and moved out to the countryside as well. As made evident in the text, the Cobbs were socialites, and their converted barn home served well to raise a family and host guests for the nearly four years they were forced to reside there (due to building materials and labor scarcities during the first world war preventing completion of their country home). Elisabeth Cobb, their daughter, fondly remembered the barn home as a place of

> Architectural peculiarity [which] gave it a certain air of being beleaguered, as though it were fighting with its back against the wall. It had no graces and few virtues except that it had been made originally of strong materials with honest workmanship. But how it received a new rakish roof, a circling of window boxes afroth with pink geraniums, a sassy balcony and in back … a garden … to make the most delicious little outdoor room imaginable. (172)

The Cobbs took great pleasure in planning out their farm home, and Elisabeth insists that her parents were happiest when planning where to build it, perhaps even happier than in the years they spent living in the home they did eventually build. Laura, Cobb's wife, accompanied her husband on hikes to pick the perfect spot for their home, scenes which Elisabeth remembered fondly. Scenes of her parents "perched on a rock pile in the pouring rain, quite oblivious of wet, weariness, or weather, happily arguing about the place for the yet-to-be broom closet. Should it go here, or on maturer thought, here?" made up some of the best memories of her parents (171).

Eventually the family did move into their finished country home, with many compromises made to the original plan to satisfy both their nosy friends' suggestions (or rather, their demands) and the needs and whims of the family. Cobb swears to his readers in *The Abandoned Farmers* that he and his wife, Laura, compromised on converting the smoke house into a summer house with an attached pergola to serve both Laura's interests in sitting outside and serving tea in the afternoons and Irvin's own desire to have a private study. In fact, no such compromise was actually made. Irvin converted the ice house to his own personal study. What became of the summer house and pergola idea is

An Introduction in Disguise   xv

lost to history. Only one thing is for certain: it did not exist at the actual Rebel Ridge estate (Lawson 147–48).

The Abandoned Farmers was published in 1920 by George H. Doran Company of New York and was sold for $3.00 a copy ("In a Lighter Vein 164"). Before it was published in full, however, Cobb first played with the idea of an abandoned farm story in 1909 when he published a short piece, "'Larry, Did You Ever Stay at an Abandoned Farm?' Asks the Hotel Clerk" in the *St. Louis Dispatch*. He later published what would become chapter two of the finished, full-length 1920 text as "Life Among the Abandoned Farmers" in *The Saturday Evening Post* in 1913 (Lawson 145). Cobb then again published this same, shorter story in his collection, *The Works of Irvin S. Cobb: Those Times and These* in 1917. This version of the story is very similar to that of the full-length reproduced chapter two, which would finally appear in the 1920 *The Abandoned Farmers*. For the most part, the 1917 version and the 1920 version are identical, with a few minor grammatical and formatting changes. The only real differences between the two are at the beginning and end of the story. Cobb begins his 1917 version with the following opening paragraph:

> I wish to say I have given up all intention of buying an abandoned farm. This decision on my part is fixed and irrevocable. I arrived at it after a long period of study and investigation. Much as I regret to state it, I shall never live on an abandoned farm and be an abandoned farmer. ("Life Among" 343)

This paragraph does not exist in the 1920 version. Of course we learn in the 1920 edition that Cobb does succeed at becoming a so-called abandoned farmer. So much for his "fixed and irrevocable" decision.

The 1917 story closes with two additional paragraphs (both nonexistent in the 1920 version):

> So, as I said at the outset, I have definitely given up my purpose of buying an abandoned farm and becoming an abandoned farmer. This spring we began looking about the Upper West Side for an abandoned flat.
>
> Judging by the entrance halls and the interior decorations in the new buildings we have visited thus far,

they are probably the most abandoned flats in the world. ("Life Among" 374).

Sounds like a housing crisis to me.
 The paper trail reflecting the reception of *The Abandoned Farmers* is scant, but it appears the book was met with mixed reviews. On the positive side, reviewers seemed to grasp that Cobb's latest work was both a how-to tale of taking flight out of the city to the country *and* a book of humor. In a Sunday *New York Times* book review, a large square of space is dedicated to *The Abandoned Famers*, set right above the so-named "greatest book of the year," modernist heavyweight author H.G. Wells' *The Outline of History: Being a Plain History of Life and Mankind*. The review for *The Abandoned Farmers*, nestled in close to H.G. Wells' lauded triumph, is favorable, calling the book "genuine" and Cobb's humor "a stimulus to every man who, tired of noises and extra nervous pressure, would find him a dwelling far from the maddening crowd." Other reviews praise Cobb for portraying "all the painful experiences of the site-seeker, the post-war home builder, the collector of antiques, and the amateur poultry fancier" while staying true to the "hilarious chapters, full of such exaggerations and delicious absurdities, and homely allusions" his fans expect, but, notably, "never vainly" ("Hard Times"). This reviewer from the *The Courier-Journal* (Louisville, Kentucky) aptly picks up on the advice and guidebook tone of *The Abandoned Farmers*. For, there is indeed "some genuine enthusiasm for home-making and some advice that may well prove valuable to would-be 'abandoned farmers'" ("Hard Times"). But, readers of this particular newspaper column are warned, or rather reminded, Cobb is a wealthy man, a successful author, journalist, and actor. It would do the *Courier-Journal*'s readers well to remember "the very thought of a farm must be abandoned, except by millionaires and successful authors." But never fret, "there is fun enough [in the book] to salve the possible disappointment" ("Hard Times").
 On the negative side of the review coin, one unnamed reviewer for the journal *America* writes, "The humor in professedly funny books often grows thin and Mr. Cobb's is not free from the blemish" ("In a Lighter Vein" 164). Another, Henry Christeen Warnack, a rancher turned theatre reviewer for the *The LA Times*, pokes fun at Cobb for his seemingly naive, boastful pride of owning a farm, calling him out on his lack of *real* farming skill: "Not Irvin S. Cobb himself had anything on me as an abandoned farmer, excepting that Cobb has to pay taxes where

he works and gets nothing out of the pay-roll for himself, whereas, in my case, another man paid the taxes and I got wages" (18).

Perhaps Cobb's tongue-in-cheek humor, his sarcastic comments on the state of modernized city folk, and his blasé frustrations with the task of building Rebel Ridge are not the witty wordplay of American writers and humorists like Mark Twain and O. Henry. Perhaps they offend the traditional agricultural laborer. But, I argue, the book's naivete about farming is its primary appeal and makes for excellent jokes. (Who else would laugh at a failing farm but a well-to-do writer?) The humor, furthermore, lacks that distinctive American humorist quality because it revels in its character's inferiority. But Cobb instead achieves something as novel, from the standpoint of literary criticism, as those humorous predecessors before him: Cobb is the torchbearer for an American standard of agrarian or country-set humor that we still see today in television, movies, novels, and nonfiction essays.

Already achieved by British authors such as Oscar Wilde in *The Importance of Being Earnest* (1895) and P.G. Wodehouse in *Blandings Castle* series (1915–77), the countryside is portrayed as a place where farce, comedy, and utter nonsense can reign supreme. The city, however, is where traffic jams, technology, uptight manners, and modernized culture govern the day. When the city goes to the country, humor has its "hay day."

What is a farm, anyway? Is it a place of pastoral, idyllic landscape? A place evoking nostalgia for an earlier, more peaceful, hard-working time? Or is it a place for comic misadventures? Where colorful characters like Chevy Chase in the movie *Funny Farm* (1988) flail about and fail at farming? Where a city couple in *Green Acres* (1965–71) struggles with the new lifestyle of the countryside and earns the boisterous laughs of their neighbors and friends?

Irvin S. Cobb's *The Abandoned Farmers* is nonfiction comedy. Although it does recount the family's search for a country home, Cobb portrays their adventure as a humorous one. He could have easily made *The Abandoned Farmers* a simple how-not-to move to the countryside tale. A book of complaints. A book recalling the epic adventures and burdensome trials of domestic dispute over planning and designing a house with your spouse. Instead, Cobb does the opposite. For Cobb himself said of humor,

> There is nothing very cultured or esthetic about a sense of humor … To me it seems a philosophic sense of vulgarity.… However, all humor is based on tragedy. Humor is really a contradiction of verities. It's actually a sober fact standing on its head and performing tricks for the benefits of the spectators. (qtd in Harrison 8–9)

Character downfalls and pitfalls are the kindling for flickers of laughter in this book. The truths of how to run an abandoned farm are turned upside down with each mistake, with each animal obscenity, with each human blunder. The farming scene, the countryside, and the farmers themselves—both the original rural folk of the region and those city dwellers turned "gentlemen farmers"—are sites of funny exposé, satire, and misfortune as Cobb and his family adjust to the farming lifestyle. The farm—a place where Cobb's "philosophic sense of vulgarity" reigns supreme—would, of course, serve as the perfect setting for Irvin S. Cobb's brand of humor.

Are farms funny? If you find obstinate, egg-barren country fowl; antics of gentlemen farmers intent on their farming experiments; and hoodlum, feral barn cats' determined meows of distaste for their new human neighbors as amusing as I do, perhaps you too would agree with my summary of this book: well, it's rather a funny story …

Works Cited

"'The Abandoned Farmers,' Cobb." Review of Irvin S. Cobb's *The Abandoned Farmers*. *Oakland Tribune* (Oakland, CA), 5 Dec. 1920, p. 4-D, c. 7. Newspapers.com.

"Among the New Books: Miscellaneous," *Detroit Free Press* (Detroit, MI), 28 Nov. 1920.

Bercaw, Louis Oldham and Annie M. Hannay. *Bibliography on Land Utilization, 1918–1936*. Washington, DC: United States Department of Agriculture, 1938.

Chatterton, Wayne. *Irvin S. Cobb*. Boston: Twayne Publishers, 1986.

Cobb, Elisabeth. *My Wayward Parent: A Book about Irvin S. Cobb*. Indianapolis, IN: The Bobbs-Merrill Company, 1945.

Cobb, Irvin S. *The Abandoned Farmers: His Humorous Account of a Retreat from the City to the Country*. Hastings, NE: Hastings College Press, 2016.

———. *Exit Laughing*. Indianapolis, IN: The Bobbs-Merrill Company, 1941.

———. "Fiction Characters, Irvin Cobb's Week-End Guests." *San Antonio Express*, 24 Feb. 1924, 15.

———. "'Larry, Did You Ever Stay at an Abandoned Farm?' Asks the Hotel Clerk." *St. Louis Dispatch*, 22 Aug. 1909, 9. Newspapers.com.

———. "Life Among the Abandoned Farmers." *The Works of Irvin S. Cobb: Those Times and These*. New York: George H. Doran Company, 1917: 343–74.

Dietrich, John and Susan Dietrich. "Irvin Cobb Cabins." IrvinCobbResort.com.

Drew, Bernard A. "Irvin S. Cobb (1876–1944): Jeff Poindexter." In *Black Stereotypes in Popular Series Fiction, 1951–1955: Jim Crow Era Authors and Their Characters*, 77–88. Jefferson, NC: McFarland & Company, 2015.

Eder, Bruce. "Irvin S. Cobb Biography." Fandango.com.

Grinnell, James W. "Irvin S. Cobb (Book)." Review of *Irvin S. Cobb*, by Anita Lawson. *Studies in Short Fiction* vol. 22 (Spring 1985): 251–52.

"Hard Times for Major Gloom." Review of Irvin S. Cobb's *The Abandoned Farmers*. *The Courier-Journal* (Louisville, KY), 12 Dec. 1920, p. 10, c. 2. Newspapers.com.

Harrison, Henry. "Famous Humorists are Really Serious Thinkers." *The Brooklyn Daily Eagle* (Brooklyn, NY), 21 June 1925, 8–9. Newspapers.com.

Holth, Nathan, Rick McOmber, and Luke Gordon. "Brookport Bridge: Irvin S. Cobb Bridge." Historicbridges.org.

Hoover, Judith D. "Irvin S. Cobb: A Rhetorical Biography." PhD Diss, Indiana University, 1983.

"Hotel Irvin Cobb—Paducah, Kentucky—U.S. National Register of Historic Places." waymarking.com.

"In a Lighter Vein." *America* vol. 24, no. 7 (4 Dec. 1920): 164. Humanities Source, EBSCOhost.

"Irvin S. Cobb." IMDB.com.

"Irvin S. Cobb Inner Cigar Box Label." Vintage-cratelabels.com.

Laut, A.C. "Ready-Made Farms." *The Country Gentleman*, 9 Nov. 1912, 3–4. Google Books.

Lawson, Anita. *Irvin S. Cobb*. Bowling Green, OH: Bowling Green University Press, 1984.

Rev. of Irvin S. Cobb's *The Abandoned Farmers: His Humorous Account of a Retreat from the City to the Farm*. *The New York Times Book Review and Magazine*, 7 Nov. 1920, p. 24, c. 4. Newspapers.com.

Rodell, Besha. "What We're Reading: *Irvin S. Cobb's Own Recipe Book* + A Cocktail Recipe." *LA Weekly*, 17 Sep. 2012.

T.W. "Introducing Irvin S. Cobb 'Back Home' at Macauley's." *The Courier-Journal* (Louisville, KY), 14 Feb. 1915, p. 4, col. 3–5. Newspapers.com.

Warnack, Henry Christeen. "Hollywood Discovers the Community Theater." *The Los Angeles Times*, 11 Nov. 1917, 18. Newspapers.com.

....

Hannah M. Biggs is a PhD candidate in English at Rice University. She also serves as a faculty member at The Women's Institute of Houston, an adult continuing-education center. Her dissertation, "Regional, Agrarian Modernisms: Farming Fiction and Rural Modernity in 20th-century British and American Prose," explores the role of agrarian settings in both high modernist and popular modernist-era novels while detailing the complicated, posthumanist relationships between the farmer, Edwardian estate gentleman, and other humans with their farm animals. Hannah's work has, or will, appear in *The F. Scott Fitzgerald Review*, *Amerikastudien / American Studies*, *Midwestern Miscellany*, and *Middle West Review*. She is also the proud doggy parent to four rescue dogs and is an avid equestrian.

I

Which Really Is a Preface in Disguise

It is the inclination of the average reader to skip prefaces. For this I do not in the least blame him. Skipping the preface is one of my favorite literary pursuits. To catch me napping a preface must creep up quietly and take me, as it were, unawares.

But in this case sundry prefatory remarks became necessary. It was essential that they should be inserted into this volume in order that certain things might be made plain. The questions were: How and where? After giving the matter considerable thought I decided to slip them in right here, included, as they are, with the body of the text and further disguised by masquerading themselves under a chapter heading, with a view in mind of hoodwinking you into pursuing the course of what briefly I have to say touching on the circumstances attending the production of the main contents. Let me explain:

Chapter II, coming immediately after this one, was written first of all; written as an independent contribution to American letters. At the time of writing it I had no thought that out of it, subsequently, would grow material for additional and supplementary offerings upon the same general theme and inter-related themes. It had a basis of verity, as all things in this life properly should have, but I shall not attempt to deny that largely it deals with what more or less is figurative and fanciful. The incident of the finding of the missing will in the ruins of the old mill is a pure figment of the imagination; so, too, the passage relating to the search for the lost heir and the startling outcome of that search (p. 36).

Three years later, actual events in the meantime having sufficiently justified the taking of such steps, I prepared the matter which here is presented in Chapters III, IV and V, inclusive. Intervened then a break of approximately two years more, when the tale was completed substantially in its present form. In all of these latter installments I adhered closely to facts, merely adding here and there sprinklings of fancy, like dashes of paprika on a stew, in order to give, as I fondly hoped, spice to my recital.

One of the prime desires now, in consolidating the entire narrative within these covers, is to round out, from inception to finish, the record of our strange adventures in connection with our quest for an abandoned farm and on our becoming abandoned farmers, trusting that others, following our examples, may perhaps profit in some small degree by our mistakes as here set forth and perhaps ultimately when their dreams have come true, too, share in that proud joy of possession which is ours. Another object, largely altruistic in its nature, is to afford opportunity for the reader, by comparison of the chronological sub-divisions into which the story falls, to decide whether with the passage of time, my style of writing shows a tendency toward improvement or an increasing and enhanced faultiness. Those who feel inclined to write me upon the subject are notified that the author is most sensible in this regard, being ever ready to welcome criticism, provided only the criticism be favorable in tone. Finally there is herewith confessed a third motive, namely, an ambition that a considerable number of persons may see their way clear to buy this book.

Quite aside from my chief aim as a writer, which is from time to time to enrich our native literature, I admit to sharing with nearly all writers and with practically all publishers a possibly selfish but not altogether unnatural craving. When I have prepared the material for a volume I desire that the volume may sell, which means royalties, which means cash in hand. The man who labors for art's sake alone nearly always labors for art's sake alone; at least usually he appears to get very little else out of his toil while he is alive. After his death posterity may enshrine him, but posterity, as some one has aptly said, butters no parsnips. I may state that I am almost passionately fond of my parsnips, well-buttered. My publisher is also one of our leading parsnip-lovers. These facts should be borne in mind by prospective purchasers of the book.

I believe that is about all I would care to say in the introductory phase. With these few remarks, therefore, the attention of the reader respectfully is directed to Chapter II and points beyond.

II

The Start of a Dream

For years it was the dream of our life—I should say our lives, since my wife shared this vision with me—to own an abandoned farm. The idea first came to us through reading articles that appeared in the various magazines and newspapers telling of the sudden growth of what I may call the abandoned-farm industry.

It seemed that New England in general—and the state of Connecticut in particular—was thickly speckled with delightful old places which, through overcultivation or ill-treatment, had become for the time being sterile and nonproductive; so that the original owners had moved away to the nearby manufacturing towns, leaving their ancestral homesteads empty and their ancestral acres idle. As a result there were great numbers of desirable places, any one of which might be had for a song. That was the term most commonly used by the writers of these articles—abandoned farms going for a song. Now, singing is not my forte; still, I made up my mind that if such indeed was the case I would sing a little, accompanying myself on my bank balance, and win me an abandoned farm.

The formula as laid down by the authorities was simple in the extreme: Taking almost any Connecticut town for a starting point, you merely meandered along an elm-lined road until you came to a desirable location, which you purchased for the price of the aforesaid song. This formality being completed, you spent a trivial sum in restoring the fences, and so on, and modernizing the interior of the house; after which it was a comparatively easy task to restore the land to productiveness by processes of intensive agriculture—details procurable from any standard book on the subject or through easy lessons by mail. And so presently, with scarcely any trouble or expense at all, you were the possessor of a delightful country estate upon which to spend your declining years. It made no difference whether you were one of those persons who had never to date declined anything of value; there was no telling when you might start in.

I could shut my eyes and see the whole delectable prospect: Upon a gentle eminence crowned with ancient trees stood the rambling old manse, filled with marvelous antique furniture, grandfather's clocks dating back to the whaling days, spinning wheels, pottery that came over on the *Mayflower*, and all those sorts of things. Round about were the meadows, some under cultivation and some lying fallow, the latter being dotted at appropriate intervals with fallow deer.

At one side of the house was the orchard, the old gnarly trees crooking their bent limbs as though inviting one to come and pluck the sun-kissed fruit from the burdened bough; at the other side a purling brook wandering its way into a greenwood copse, where through all the golden day sang the feathered warblers indigenous to the climate, including the soft-billed Greenwich thrush, the Peabody bird, the Pettingill bird, the red worsted pulse-warmer, and others of the commoner varieties too numerous to mention.

At the back were the abandoned cotes and byres, with an abandoned rooster crowing lustily upon a henhouse, and an abandoned bull calf disporting himself in the clover of the pasture. At the front was a rolling vista undulating gently away to where above the tree-tops there rose the spires of a typical New England village full of old line Republicans and characters suitable for putting into short stories. On beyond, past where a silver lake glinted in the sunshine, was a view either of the distant Sound or the distant mountains. Personally I intended that my establishment should be so placed as to command a view of the Sound from the east windows and of the mountains from the west windows. And all to be had for a song! Why, the mere thought of it was enough to make a man start taking vocal culture right away.

Besides, I had been waiting impatiently for a long time for an opportunity to work out several agricultural projects of my own. For example, there was my notion in regard to the mulberry. The mulberry, as all know, is one of our most abundant small fruits; but many have objected to it on account of its woolly appearance and slightly caterpillary taste. My idea was to cross the mulberry on the slippery elm—pronounced, where I came from, ellum—producing a fruit which I shall call the mulellum. This fruit would combine the health-giving qualities of the mulberry with the agreeable smoothness of the slippery elm; in fact, if my plans worked out I should have a berry that would go down so slick the consumer could not taste it at all unless he should eat too many of them and suffer from indigestion afterward.

Then there was my scheme for inducing the common chinch bug to make chintz curtains. If the silk worms can make silk why should not the chinch bug do something useful instead of wasting his energies in idle pursuits? This is what I wished to know. And why should this man Luther Burbank enjoy a practical monopoly of all these propositions? That was the way I looked at it; and I figured

The Start of a Dream

that an abandoned farm would make an ideal place for working out such experiments as might come to me from time to time.

The trouble was that, though everybody wrote of the abandoned farms in a broad, general, alluring way, nobody gave the exact location of any of them. I subscribed for one of the monthly publications devoted to country life along the Eastern seaboard and searched assiduously through its columns for mention of abandoned farms. The owners of most of the country places that were advertised for sale made mention of such things as fourteen master's bedrooms and nine master's baths—showing undoubtedly that the master would be expected to sleep oftener than he bathed—sunken gardens and private hunting preserves, private golf links and private yacht landings.

In nearly every instance, also, the advertisement was accompanied by a halftone picture of a structure greatly resembling the new county court house they are going to have down at Paducah if the bond issue ever passes. This seemed a suitable place for holding circuit court in, or even fiscal court, but it was not exactly the kind of country home that we had pictured for ourselves. As my wife said, just the detail of washing all those windows would keep the girl busy fully half the time. Nor did I care to invest in any sunken gardens. I had sufficient experience in that direction when we lived in the suburbs and permanently invested about half of what I made in our eight-by-ten flower bed in an effort to make it produce the kind of flowers that the florists' catalogues described. You could not tell us anything about that subject—we knew where a sunken garden derives its name. We paid good money to know.

None of the places advertised in the monthly seemed sufficiently abandoned for our purposes, so for a little while we were in a quandary. Then I had a bright thought. I said to myself that undoubtedly abandoned farms were so cheap the owners did not expect to get any real money for them; they would probably be willing to take something in exchange. So I began buying the evening papers and looking through them in the hope of running across some such item as this:

> To Exchange—Abandoned farm, centrally located, with large farmhouse, containing all antique furniture, barns, outbuildings, family graveyard—planted—orchard, woodland, fields—unplanted—for a collection of postage stamps in album, an amateur magician's outfit, a guitar with book of instructions, a safety bicycle, or what have you? Address ABANDONED, South Squantum Center, Connecticut.

I found no such offers, however; and in view of what we had read this seemed stranger still. Finally I decided that the only safe method would be by first-hand investigation upon the spot. I would go by rail to some small but accessible hamlet in the lower part of New England. On arriving there I personally would examine a number of the more attractive abandoned farms in the immediate vicinity and make a discriminating selection. Having reached this conclusion I went to bed and slept peacefully—or at least I went to bed and did so as soon as my wife and I had settled one point that came up unexpectedly at this juncture. It related to the smokehouse. I was in favor of turning the smokehouse into a study or workroom for myself. She thought, though, that by knocking the walls out and altering the roof and building a pergola on to it, it would make an ideal summer house in which to serve tea and from which to view the peaceful landscape of afternoons.

We argued this back and forth at some length, each conceding something to the other's views; and finally we decided to knock out the walls and alter the roof and have a summer house with a pergola in connection. It was after we reached this compromise that I slept so peacefully, for now the whole thing was as good as settled. I marveled at not having thought of it sooner.

It was on a bright and peaceful morning that I alighted from the train at North Newburybunkport. Considering that it was supposed to be a typical New England village, North Newburybunkport did not appear at first glance to answer to the customary specifications, such as I had gleaned from my reading of novels of New England life. I had expected that the platform would be populated by picturesque natives in quaint clothes, with straws in their mouths and all whittling; and that the depot agent would wear long chin whiskers and say "I vum!" with much heartiness at frequent intervals. Right here I wish to state that so far as my observations go the native who speaks these words about every other line is no longer on the job. Either I Vum the Terrible has died or else he has gone to England to play the part of the typical American millionaire in American plays written by Englishmen.

Instead of the loafers, several chauffeurs were idling about the station and a string of automobiles was drawn up across the road. Just as I disembarked there drove up a large red bus labeled: Sylvan Dale Summer Hotel, European and American Plans. The station agent also proved in the nature of a disappointment. He did not even say "I swan" or "I cal'late!" or anything of that nature. He wore a pink in his buttonhole and his hair was scalloped up off his forehead in what is known as the lion tamer's roach. Approaching, I said to him:

"In what direction should I go to find some of the abandoned farms of this vicinity? I would prefer to go where there is a good assortment to pick from."

He did not appear to understand, so I repeated the question, at the same time offering him a cigar.

"Bo," he said, "you've sure got me winging now. You'd better ask Tony Magnito—he runs the garage three doors up the street from here on the other side. Tony does a lot of driving round the country for suckers that come up here, and he might help you."

To reach the garage I had to cross the road, dodging several automobiles in transit, and then pass two old-fashioned New England houses fronting close up to the sidewalk. One had the sign of a teahouse over the door, and in the window of the other, picture postcards, birch-bark souvenirs and standard varieties of candy were displayed for sale.

Despite his foreign-sounding name, Mr. Magnito spoke fair English—that is, as fair English as any one speaks who employs the Manhattan accent in so doing.

Even after he found out that I did not care to rent a touring car for sightseeing purposes at five dollars an hour he was quite affable and accommodating; but my opening question appeared to puzzle him just as in the case of the depot agent.

"Mister," he said frankly, "I'm sorry, but I don't seem to make you. What's this thing you is looking for? Tell me over again slow."

Really the ignorance of these villagers regarding one of their principal products—a product lying, so to speak, at their very doors and written about constantly in the public prints—was ludicrous. It would have been laughable if it had not been deplorable. I saw that I could not indulge in general trade terms. I must be painfully explicit and simple.

"What I am seeking"—I said it very slowly and very distinctly—"is a farm that has been deserted, so to speak—one that has outlived its usefulness as a farm proper, and everything like that!"

"Oh," he says, "now I get you! Why didn't you say that in the first place? The place you're looking for is the old Parham place, out here on the post road about a mile. August'll take good care of you—that's his specialty."

"August?" I inquired. "August who?"

"August Weinstopper—the guy who runs it," he explained. "You must have known August if you lived long in New York. He used to be the steward at that big hotel at Broadway and Forty-second; that was before he came up here and opened up the old Parham place as an automobile roadhouse. He's cleaning up about a thousand a month. Some class to that mantrap! They've got an orchestra, and nothing but vintage goods on the wine card, and dancing at all hours. Any night you'll see forty or fifty big cars rolling up there, bringing swell dames and—"

I judge he saw by my expression that he was on a totally wrong tack, because he stopped short.

"Say, mister," he said, "I guess you'd better step into the post-office here—next door—and tell your troubles to Miss Plummer. She knows everything that's going on round here—and she ought to, too, seeing as she gets first chance at all the circulars and postal cards that come in. Besides, I gotter be changing that gasoline sign—gas has went up two cents a gallon more."

Miss Plummer was sorting mail when I appeared at her wicket. She was one of those elderly, spinsterish-looking, kittenish females who seem in an intense state of surprise all the time. Her eyebrows arched like croquet wickets and her mouth made O's before she uttered them.

"Name, please?" she said twitteringly.

I told her.

"Ah," she said in the thrilled tone of one who is watching a Fourth of July skyrocket explode in midair. The news seemed to please her.

"And the initials, please?"

"The initials are of no consequence. I do not expect any mail," I said. "I want merely to ask you a question."

"Indeed!" she said coyly. She said it as though I had just given her a handsome remembrance, and she cocked her head on one side like a bird—like a hen-bird.

"I hate to trouble you," I went on, "but I have experienced some difficulty in making your townspeople understand me. I am looking for a certain kind of farm—a farm of an abandoned character."

At once I saw I had made a mistake.

"You do not get my meaning," I said hastily. "I refer to a farm that has been deserted, closed up, shut down—in short, abandoned. I trust I make myself plain."

Chapter II

She was still suffering from shock, however. She gave me a wounded-fawn glance and averted her burning face.

"The Prewitt property might suit your purposes—whatever they may be," she said coldly over her shoulder. "Mr. Jabez Pickerel, of Pickerel & Pike, real-estate dealers, on the first corner above, will doubtless give you the desired information. He has charge of the Prewitt property."

At last, I said to myself as I turned away, I was on the right track. Mr. Pickerel rose as I entered his place of business. He was a short, square man, with a brisk manner and a roving eye.

"I have been directed to you," I began. He seized my hand and began shaking it warmly. "I have been told," I continued, "that you have charge of the old Prewitt farm somewhere near here; and as I am in the market for an aban—" I got no farther than that.

"In one minute," he shouted explosively—"in just one minute!"

Still clutching me by the hand, he rushed me pell-mell out of the place. At the curbing stood a long, low, rakish racing-model roadster, looking something like a high-powered projectile and something like an enlarged tailor's goose. Leaping into this machine at one bound, he dragged me up into the seat beside him and threw on the power. Instantly we were streaking away at a perfectly appalling rate of speed—fully forty-five to fifty-five miles an hour I should say. You never saw anything so sudden in your life. It was exactly like a kidnapping. It was only by the exercise of great self-control that I restrained myself from screaming for help. I had the feeling that I was being abducted—for what purpose I knew not.

As we spun round a corner on two wheels, spraying up a long furrow of dust, the same as shown in pictures of the chariot race in Ben-Hur, a man with a watch in his hand and wearing a badge—a constable, I think—ran out of a house that had a magistrate's sign over it and threw up his hand authoritatively, as though to stop us; but my companion yelled something the purport of which I could not distinguish and the constable fell back. Glancing rearward over my shoulder I saw him halting another car bearing a New York license that did not appear to be going half so fast as we were.

In another second we were out of town, tearing along a country highway. Evidently sensing the alarm expressed by my tense face and strained posture, this man Pickerel began saying something in what was evidently intended to be a reassuring tone; but such was the roaring of the car that I could distinguish only broken fragments of his speech. I caught the words "unparalleled opportunity," repeated several times—the term appeared to be a favorite of his—and "marvelous proposition." Possibly I was not listening very closely anyhow, my mind being otherwise engaged. For one thing I was surmising in a general sort of way upon the old theory of the result when the irresistible force encounters the immovable object. I was wondering how long it would be before we hit something solid and whether it would be possible afterward to tell us apart. His straw hat also made me wonder. I had mine clutched in both hands and even then it fluttered against my bosom like a captive bird, but his stayed put. I think yet he must have had threads cut in his head to match the convolutions of the straw and screwed his hat on, like a nut on an axle.

I have a confused recollection of rushing with the speed of the tornado through rows of trees; of leaping from the crest of one small hill to the crest of the next small hill; of passing a truck patch with such velocity that the lettuce and tomatoes and other things all seemed to merge together in a manner suggestive of a well-mixed vegetable salad. Then we swung off the main road in between the huge brick columns of an ornate gateway that stood alone, with no fence in connection. We bumpily traversed a rutted stretch of cleared land; and then with a jar and a jolt we came to a pause in what appeared to be a wide and barren expanse.

As my heart began to throb with slightly less violence I looked about me for the abandoned farmhouse. I had conceived that it would be white with green blinds and that it would stand among trees. It was not in sight; neither were the trees. The entire landscape presented an aspect that was indeed remarkable. Small numbered stakes, planted in double lines at regular intervals, so as to form aisles, stretched away from us in every direction. Also there were twin rows of slender sticks planted in the earth in a sort of geometric pattern. Some were the size of switches. Others were almost as large as umbrella handles and had sprouted slightly. A short distance away an Italian was steering a dirtscraper attached to a languid mule along a sort of dim roadway. There were no other living creatures in sight. Right at my feet were two painted and lettered boards affixed at cross angles to a wooden upright. The legend on one of these boards was: Grand Concourse. The inscription on the other read: Nineteenth Avenue West. Repressing a gasp, I opened my mouth to speak.

"Ahem!" I said. "There has been some mistake—"

"There can be no mistake!" he shouted enthusiastically. "The only mistake possible is not to take advantage of this magnificent opportunity while it is yet possible to do so. Just observe that view!" He waved his arm in the general direction of the horizon from northwest to southeast. "Breathe this air! As a personal favor to me just breathe a little of this air!" He inhaled deeply himself as though to show me how, and I followed suit, because after that ride I needed to catch up with my regular breathing.

"Thank you!" I said gratefully when I had finished breathing. "But how about—"

"Quite right!" he cried, beaming upon me admiringly. "Quite right! I don't blame you. You have a right to know all the details. As a business man you should ask that question. You were about to say: But how about the train service? Ah, there spoke the true business man, the careful investor! Twenty fast trains a day each way—twenty, sir! Remember! And as for accessibility—well, accessibility is simply no name for it! Only two or three minutes from the station. You saw how long it took us to get here to-day? Well, then, what more could you ask? Right here," he went on, pointing, "is the country club—a magnificent thing!"

I looked, but I didn't see anything except a hole in the ground about fifty feet from us.

"Where?" I asked. "I don't see it."

"Well," he said, "this is where it is going to be. You automatically become a member of the country club; in fact, you are as good as a member now! And right up there at the corner of Lincoln Boulevard and Washington Parkway, where that scraper is, is the public library—the site for it! You'll be crazy about the public library! When we get back I'll let you run over the plans for the public library while I'm fixing up the papers. Oh, my friend, how glad I am you came while there was yet time!"

I breasted the roaring torrent of his pouring language.

"One minute," I begged of him—"One minute, if you please! I am obliged to you for the interest you take in me, a mere stranger to you; but there has been a misunderstanding. I wanted to see the Prewitt place."

"This is the Prewitt place," he said.

"Yes," I said; "but where is the house? And why all this—why all these—" I indicated by a wave of my hand what I meant.

"Naturally," he explained, "the house is no longer here. We tore it away—it was old; whereas everything here will be new, modern and up-to-date. This is—or was—the Prewitt place, now better known as Homecrest Heights, the Development Ideal!" Having begun to capitalize his words, he continued to do so. "The Perfect Addition! The Suburb Superb! Away From the City's Dust and Heat! Away From Its Glamor and Clamor! Into the Open! Into the Great Out-of-Doors! Back to the Soil! Villa Plots on Easy Terms! You Furnish the Birds, We Furnish the Nest! The Place For a Business Man to Rear His Family! You Are Married? You Have a Wife? You Have Little Ones?"

"Yes," I said, "one of each—one wife and one little one."

"Ah!" he cried gladly. "One Little One—How Sweet! You Love Your Little One—Ah, Yes! Yes! You Desire to Give Your Little One a Chance? You Would Give Her Congenial Surroundings—Refined Surroundings? You Would Inculcate in Her While Young the Love of Nature?" He put an entire sentence into capitals now: "GIVE YOUR LITTLE ONE A CHANCE! THAT IS ALL I ASK OF YOU!"

He had me by both lapels. I thought he was going to kneel to me in pleading. I feared he might kiss me. I raised him to his feet. Then his manner changed—it became domineering, hectoring, almost threatening.

   I will pass briefly over the events of the succeeding hour, including our return to his lair or office. Accounts of battles where all the losses fall upon one side are rarely interesting to read about anyway. Suffice it to say that at the last minute I was saved. It was a desperate struggle though. I had offered the utmost resistance at first, but he would surely have had his way with me—only that a train pulled in bound for the city just as he was showing me, as party of the first part, where I was to sign my name on the dotted line A. Even then, weakened and worn as I was, I should probably not have succeeded in beating him off if he had not been hampered by having a fountain pen in one hand and the documents in the other. At the door he intercepted me; but I tackled him low about the body and broke through and fled like a hunted roebuck, catching the last car just as the relief train pulled out of the station. It was a close squeeze, but I made it. The thwarted Mr. Pickerel wrote me regularly for some months thereafter, making mention of My Little One in every letter; but after a while I took to sending the letters back to him unopened, and eventually he quit.

   I reached home along toward evening. I was tired, but I was not discouraged. I reported progress on the part of the committee on a permanent site, but told my wife that in order to find exactly what we wanted it would be necessary for us to leave the main-traveled paths. It was now quite apparent to me that the abandoned farm-seeker who stuck too closely to the railroad lines was bound to be thrown constantly in contact with those false and feverish metropolitan influences which, radiating from the city, have spread over the country like the spokes of a wheel or an upas tree, or a jauganaut, or something of that nature. The thing to do was to get into an automobile and go away from the principal routes of travel, into districts where the abandoned farms would naturally be more numerous.

This solved one phase of the situation—we now knew definitely where to go. The next problem was to decide upon some friend owning an automobile. We fixed upon the Winsells. They are charming people! We are devoted to the Winsells. They were very good friends of ours when they had their small four-passenger car; but since they sold the old one and bought a new forty-horse, seven-passenger car, they are so popular that it is hard to get hold of them for holidays and week-ends.

Every Saturday—nearly—some one of their list of acquaintances is calling them up to tell of a lovely spot he has just heard about, with good roads all the way, both coming and going; but after a couple of disappointments we caught them when they had an open date. Over the telephone Winsell objected that he did not know anything about the roads up in Connecticut, but I was able to reassure him promptly on that score. I told him he need not worry about that—that I would buy the road map myself. So on a fair Saturday morning we started.

The trip up through the extreme lower end of the state of New York was delightful, being marred by only one or two small mishaps. There was the trifling incident of a puncture, which delayed us slightly; but fortunately the accident occurred at a point where there was a wonderful view of the Croton Lakes, and while Winsell was taking off the old tire and adjusting a new one we sat very comfortably in the car, enjoying Nature's panorama.

It was a little later on when we hit a dog. It seemed to me that this dog merely sailed, yowling, up into the air in a sort of long curve, but Winsell insisted that the dog described a parabola. I am very glad that in accidents of this character it is always the victims that describe the parabola. I know I should be at a complete loss to describe one myself. Unless it is something like the boomerang of the Australian aborigines I do not even know what a parabola is. Nor did I dream until then that Winsell understood the dog language. However, those are but technical details.

After we crossed the state line we got lost several times; this was because the country seemed to have a number of roads the road map omitted, and the road map had many roads the country had left out. Eventually, though, we came to a district of gently rolling hills, dotted at intervals with those neat white-painted villages in which New England excels; and between the villages at frequent intervals were farmhouses. Abandoned ones, however, were rarer than we had been led to expect. Not only were these farms visibly populated by persons who appeared to be permanently attached to their respective localities, but at many of them things were offered for sale—such as home-made pastry, souvenirs, fresh poultry, antique furniture, brass door-knockers, milk and eggs, hand-painted crockery, table board, garden truck, molasses taffy, laundry soap and livestock.

At length, though, when our necks were quite sore from craning this way and that on the watch for an abandoned farm that would suit us, we came to a very attractive-looking place facing a lawn and flanked by an orchard. There was a sign fastened to an elm tree alongside the fence. The sign read: For Information Concerning This Property Inquire Within.

To Winsell I said:

"Stop here—this is without doubt the place we have been looking for!"

Filled—my wife and I—with little thrills of anticipation, we all got out. I opened the gate and entered the yard, followed by Winsell, my wife and his wife. I was about halfway up the walk when a large dog sprang into view, at the same time showing his teeth in rather an intimidating way. To prevent an encounter with an animal that might be hostile, I stepped nimbly behind the nearest tree. As I came round on the other side of the tree there, to my surprise, was this dog face to face with me. Still desiring to avoid a collision with him, I stepped back the other way. Again I met the dog, which was now growling. The situation was rapidly becoming embarrassing when a gentleman came out upon the porch and called sharply to the dog. The dog, with apparent reluctance, retired under the house and the gentleman invited us inside and asked us to be seated. Glancing about his living room I noted that the furniture appeared to be a trifle modern for our purposes; but, as I whispered to my wife, you cannot expect to have everything to suit you at first. With the sweet you must ever take the bitter—that I believe is true, though not an original saying.

In opening the conversation with the strange gentleman I went in a businesslike way direct to the point.

"You are the owner of these premises?" I asked. He bowed. "I take it," I then said, "that you are about to abandon this farm?"

"I beg your pardon?" he said, as though confused.

"I presume," I explained, "that this is practically an abandoned farm."

"Not exactly," he said. "I'm here."

"Yes, yes; quite so," I said, speaking perhaps a trifle impatiently. "But you are thinking of going away from it, aren't you?"

"Yes," he admitted; "I am."

"Now," I said, "we are getting round to the real situation. What are you asking for this place?"

"Eighteen hundred," he stated. "There are ninety acres of land that go with the house and the house itself is in very good order."

I considered for a moment. None of the abandoned farms I had ever read about sold for so much as eighteen hundred dollars. Still, I reflected, there might have been a recent bull movement; there had certainly been much publicity upon the subject. Before committing myself, I glanced at my wife. Her expression betokened acquiescence.

"That figure," I said diplomatically, "was somewhat in excess of what I was originally prepared to pay; still, the house seems roomy and, as you were saying, there are ninety acres. The furniture and equipment go with the place, I presume?"

"Naturally," he answered. "That is the customary arrangement."

"And would you be prepared to give possession immediately?"

"Immediately," he responded.

I began to feel enthusiasm. By the look on my wife's face I could tell that she was enthused, too.

"If we come to terms," I said, "and everything proves satisfactory, I suppose you could arrange to have the deed made out at once?"

"The deed?" he said blankly. "You mean the lease?"

"The lease?" I said blankly. "You mean the deed?"

"The deed?" he said blankly. "You mean the lease?"

"The lease, indeed," said my wife. "You mean—"

I broke in here. Apparently we were all getting the habit.

"Let us be perfectly frank in this matter," I said. "Let us dispense with these evasive and dilatory tactics. You want eighteen hundred dollars for this place, furnished?"

"Exactly," he responded. "Eighteen hundred dollars for it from June to October." Then, noting the expressions of our faces, he continued hurriedly: "A remarkably small figure considering what summer rentals are in this section. Besides, this house is new. It costs a lot to reproduce these old Colonial designs!"

I saw at once that we were but wasting our time in this person's company. He had not the faintest conception of what we wanted. We came away. Besides, as I remarked to the others after we were back in the car and on our way again, this house-farm would never have suited us; the view from it was nothing extra. I told Winsell to go deeper into the country until we really struck the abandoned farm belt.

So we went farther and farther. After a while it was late afternoon and we seemed to be lost again. My wife and Winsell's wife were tired; so we dropped them at the next teahouse we passed. I believe it was the eighteenth teahouse for the day. Winsell and I then continued on the quest alone. Women know so little about business anyway that it is better, I think, whenever possible, to conduct important matters without their presence. It takes a masculine intellect to wrestle with these intricate problems; and for some reason or other this problem was becoming more and more complicated and intricate all the time.

On a long, deserted stretch of road, as the shadows were lengthening, we overtook a native of a rural aspect plodding along alone. Just as we passed him I was taken with an idea and I told Winsell to stop. I was tired of trafficking with stupid villagers and avaricious land-grabbers. I would deal with the peasantry direct. I would sound the yeoman heart—which is honest and true and ever beats in accord with the best dictates of human nature.

"My friend," I said to him, "I am seeking an abandoned farm. Do you know of many such in this vicinity?"

"How?" he asked.

I never got so tired of repeating a question in my life; nevertheless, for this yokel's limited understanding, I repeated it again.

"Well," he said at length, "whut with all these city fellers moving in here to do gentleman-farming—whatsoever that may mean—farm property has gone up until now it's wuth considerable more'n town property, as a rule. I could scursely say I know of any of the kind of farms you mention as laying round loose—no, wait a minute; I do recollect a place. It's that shack up back of the country poor farm that the supervisors used for a pest house the time the smallpox broke out. That there place is consider'bly abandoned. You might try her."

In a stern tone of voice I bade Winsell to drive on and turn in at the next farmhouse he came to. The time for trifling had passed. My mind was fixed. My jaw was also set. I know, because I set it myself. And I have no doubt there was a determined glint in my eye; in fact, I could feel the glint reflected upon my cheek.

At the next farm Winsell turned in. We passed through a stone gateway and rolled up a well-kept road toward a house we could see in glimpses through the intervening trees. We skirted several rather neat flower beds, curved round a greenhouse and came out on a stretch of lawn. I at once decided that this place would do undoubtedly. There might be alterations to make, but in the main the establishment would be satisfactory even though the house, on closer inspection, proved to be larger than it had seemed when seen from a distance.

On a signal from me Winsell halted at the front porch. Without a word I stepped out. He followed. I mounted the steps, treading with great firmness and decision, and rang the doorbell hard. A middle-aged person dressed in black, with a high collar, opened the door.

"Are you the proprietor of this place?" I demanded without any preamble. My patience was exhausted; I may have spoken sharply.

"Oh, no, sir," he said, and I could tell by his accent he was English; "the marster is out, sir."

"I wish to see him," I said, "on particular business—at once! At once, you understand—it is important!"

"Perhaps you'd better come in, sir," he said humbly. It was evident my manner, which was, I may say, almost haughty, had impressed him deeply. "If you will wait, sir, I'll have the marster called, sir. He's not far away, sir."

"Very good," I replied. "Do so!"

He showed us into a large library and fussed about, offering drinks and cigars and what-not. Winsell seemed somewhat perturbed by these attentions, but I bade him remain perfectly calm and collected, adding that I would do all the talking.

We took cigars—very good cigars they were. As they were not banded I assumed they were home grown. I had always heard that Connecticut tobacco was strong, but these specimens were very mild and pleasant. I had about decided I should put in tobacco for private consumption and grow my own cigars and cigarettes when the door opened, and a stout elderly man with side whiskers entered the room. He was in golfing costume and was breathing hard.

"As soon as I got your message I hurried over as fast as I could," he said.

"You need not apologize," I replied; "we have not been kept waiting very long."

"I presume you come in regard to the traction matter?" he ventured.

"No," I said, "not exactly. You own this place, I believe?"

"I do," he said, staring at me.

"So far, so good," I said. "Now, then, kindly tell me when you expect to abandon it."

He backed away from me a few feet, gaping. He opened his mouth and for a few moments absent-mindedly left it in that condition.

"When do I expect to do what?" he inquired.

"When," I said, "do you expect to abandon it?"

He shook his head as though he had some marbles inside of it and liked the rattling sound.

"I don't understand yet," he said, puzzled.

"I will explain," I said very patiently. "I wish to acquire by purchase or otherwise one of the abandoned farms of this state. Not having been able to find one that was already abandoned, though I believe them to be very numerous, I am looking for one that is about to be abandoned. I wish, you understand, to have the first call on it. Winsell"—I said in an aside—"quit pulling at my coat-tail! Therefore," I resumed, readdressing the man with the side whiskers, "I ask you a plain question, to wit: When do you expect to abandon this one? I expect a plain answer."

He edged a few feet nearer an electric push button which was set in the wall. He seemed flustered and distraught; in fact, almost apprehensive.

"May I inquire," he said nervously, "how you got in here?"

"Your servant admitted us," I said, with dignity.

"Yes," he said in a soothing tone; "but did you come afoot—or how?"

"I drove here in a car," I told him, though I couldn't see what difference that made.

"Merciful Heavens!" he muttered. "They do not trust you—I mean you do not drive the car yourself, do you?"

Here Winsell cut in.

"I drove the car," he said. "I—I did not want to come, but he"—pointing to me—"he insisted." Winsell is by nature a groveling soul. His tone was almost cringing.

"I see," said the gentleman, wagging his head, "I see. Sad case—very sad case! Young, too!" Then he faced me. "You will excuse me now," he said. "I wish to speak to my butler. I have just thought of several things I wish to say to him. Now in regard to abandoning this place: I do not expect to abandon this place just yet—probably not for some weeks or possibly months. In case I should decide to abandon it sooner, if you will leave your address with me I will communicate with you by letter at the institution where you may chance to be stopping at the time. I trust this will be satisfactory."

He turned again to Winsell.

"Does your—ahem—friend care for flowers?" he asked.

"Yes," said Winsell. "I think so."

"Perhaps you might show him my flower gardens as you go away," said the side-whiskered man. "I have heard somewhere that flowers have a very soothing effect sometimes in such cases—or it may have been music. I have spent thirty thousand dollars beautifying these grounds and I am really very proud of them. Show him the flowers by all means—you might even let him pick a few if it will humor him."

I started to speak, but he was gone. In the distance somewhere I heard a door slam.

Under the circumstances there was nothing for us to do except to come away. Originally I did not intend to make public mention of this incident, preferring to dismiss the entire thing from my mind; but, inasmuch as Winsell has seen fit to circulate a perverted and needlessly exaggerated version of it among our circle of friends, I feel that the exact circumstances should be properly set forth.

It was a late hour when we rejoined our wives. This was due to Winsell's stupidity in forgetting the route we had traversed after parting from them; in fact, it was nearly midnight before he found his way back to the teahouse where we left them. The teahouse had been closed for some hours then and our wives were sitting in the dark on the teahouse porch waiting for us. Really, I could not blame them for scolding Winsell; but they displayed an unwarranted peevishness toward me. My wife's display of temper was really the last straw. It was that, taken in connection with certain other circumstances, which clinched my growing resolution to let the whole project slide into oblivion. I woke her up and in so many words told her so on the way home. We arrived there shortly after daylight of the following morning.

So, as I said at the outset, we gave up our purpose of buying an abandoned farm and moved into a flat on the upper west side.

III

Three Years Elapse

I wound up the last preceding chapter of this chronicle with the statement that we had definitely given up all hope of owning an abandoned farm. After an interval of three years the time has now come to recant and to make explanation, touching on our change of heart and resolution. For at this writing I am an abandoned farmer of the most pronounced type and, with the assistance of my family, am doing my level best to convert or, as it were, evangelize one of the most thoroughly abandoned farms in the entire United States. By the same token we are also members in good standing of the Westchester County—New York—Despair Association.

The Westchester County Despair Association was founded by George Creel, who is one of our neighbors. In addition to being its founder he is its perpetual president. This association has a large and steadily growing membership. Any citybred person who moves up here among the rolling hills of our section with intent to get back to Nature, and who, in pursuance of that most laudable aim, encounters the various vicissitudes and the varied misfortunes which, it would seem, invariably do befall the amateur husbandman, is eligible to join the ranks.

If he builds a fine silo and promptly it burns down on him, as so frequently happens—silos appear to have a habit of deliberately going out of their way in order to catch afire—he joins automatically. If his new swimming pool won't hold water, or his new road won't hold anything else; if his hired help all quit on him in the busy season; if the spring freshets flood his cellar; if his springs go dry in August; if his horses succumb to one of those fatal diseases that are so popular among expensive horses; if his prize Jersey cow chokes on a turnip; if his blooded hens are so busy dying they have no time to give to laying—why, then, under any one or more of these heads he is welcomed into the fold. I may state in passing that, after an experimental test of less than six months of country life, we are eligible on several counts. However, I shall refer to those details later.

Up until last spring we had been living in the city for twelve years, with a slice of about four years out of the middle, during which we lived in one of the most suburban of suburbs. First we tried the city, then the suburb, then the city again; and the final upshot was, we decided that neither city nor suburb would do for us. In the suburb there was the daily commuting to be considered; besides, the suburb was neither city nor country, but a commingling of the drawbacks of the city and the country, with not many of the advantages of either. And the city was the city of New York.

Ours, I am sure, had been the common experience of the majority of those who move to New York from smaller communities—the experience of practically all except the group from which is recruited the confirmed and incurable New Yorker. After you move to New York it takes several months to rid you of homesickness for the place you have left; this period over, it takes several years usually to cure you of the lure of the city and restore to you the longing for the simpler and saner things.

To be sure, there is the exception. When I add this qualification I have in mind the man who wearies not of spending his evenings from eight-thirty until eleven at a tired-business-man's show; of eating tired-business-man's lunch in a lobsteria on the Great White Way from eleven-thirty P.M. until closing time; of having his toes trodden upon by other tired business men at the afternoon-dancing parlor; of twice a day, or oftener, being packed in with countless fellow tired business men in the tired cars of the tired Subway—I have him in mind, also the woman who is his ordained mate.

But, for the run of us, life in the city, within a flat, eventually gets upon our nerves; and life within the city, outside the flat, gets upon our nerves to an even greater extent. The main trouble about New York is not that it contains six million people, but that practically all of them are constantly engaged in going somewhere in such a hurry. Nearly always the place where they are going lies in the opposite direction from the place where you are going. There is where the rub comes, and sooner or later it rubs the nap off your disposition.

The everlasting shooting of the human rapids, the everlasting portages about the living whirlpools, the everlasting bucking of the human cross currents—these are the things that, in due time, turn the thoughts of the sojourner to mental pictures of peaceful fields and burdened orchards, and kind-faced cows standing knee-deep in purling brooks, and bosky dells and sylvan glades. At any rate, so our thoughts turned.

Then, too, a great many of our friends were moving to the country to live, or had already moved to the country to live. We spent week-ends at their houses; we went on house parties as their guests. We heard them babble of the excitement of raising things on the land. We thought they meant garden truck. How were we to know they also meant mortgages? At the time it did not impress us as a fact worthy of being regarded as significant that we should find a different set of servants on the premises almost every time we went to visit one of these families.

What fascinated us was the presence of fresh vegetables upon the table—not the car-sick, shopworn, wilted vegetables of the city markets, but really fresh vegetables; the new-laid eggs—after eating the other kind so long we knew they were new-laid without being told; the flower beds outside and the great bouquets of flowers inside the house; the milk that had come from a cow and not from a milkman; the home-made butter; the rich cream—and all.

We heard their tales of rising at daybreak and going forth to pick from the vines the platter of breakfast berries, still beaded with the dew. They got up at daybreak, they said, especially on account of the berry picking and the beauties of the sunrise. Having formerly been city dwellers, they had sometimes stayed up for a sunrise; but never until now had they got up for one. The novelty appealed to them tremendously and they never tired of talking of it.

In the country—so they told us—you never needed an alarm clock to rouse you at dawn. Subsequently, by personal experience, I found this to be true. You never need an alarm clock—if you keep chickens. You may not go to bed with the chickens, but you get up with them, unless you are a remarkably sound sleeper. When it comes to rousing the owner from slumber before the sun shows, the big red rooster and the little brown hen are more dependable than any alarm clock ever assembled. You might forget to wind the alarm clock. The big red rooster winds himself. You might forget to set the alarm clock. The little brown hen does her own setting; and even in cases where she doesn't, she likes to wake up about four-forty-five and converse about her intentions in the matter in a shrill and penetrating tone of voice.

It had been so long since I had lived in the country I had forgotten about the early-rising habits of barnyard fowl. I am an expert on the subject now. Only this morning there was a rooster suffering from hay fever or a touch of catarrh, or something that made him quite hoarse; and he strolled up from the chicken house to a point directly beneath my bedroom window, just as the first pink streaks of the new day were painting the eastern skies, and spent fully half an hour there clearing his throat.

But I am getting ahead of my story. More and more we found the lure of the country was enmeshing our fancies. After each trip to the country we went back to town to find that, in our absence, the flat had somehow grown more stuffy and more crowded; that the streets had become more noisy and more congested. And the outcome of it with us was as the outcome has been with so many hundreds and thousands and hundreds of thousands of others. We voted to go to the country to live.

Having reached the decision, the next thing was to decide on the site and the setting for the great adventure.

We unanimously set our faces against New Jersey, mainly because, to get from New Jersey over to New York and back again, you must take either the ferry or the tube; and if there was one thing on earth that we cared less for than the ferry it was the tube. To us it seemed that most of the desirable parts of Long Island were already preëmpted by persons of great wealth, living, so we gathered, in a state of discriminating aloofness and, as a general rule, avoiding social association with families in the humbler walks of life. Round New York the rich cannot be too careful—and seldom are. Most of them are suffering from nervous culture anyhow.

Land in the lower counties of Connecticut, along the Sound, was too expensive for us to consider moving up there. But there remained what seemed to us then and what seems to us yet the most wonderful spot for country homes of persons in moderate circumstances anywhere within the New York zone, or anywhere else, for that matter—the hill country of the northern part of Westchester County, far enough back from the Hudson River to avoid the justly famous Hudson River glare in the summer, and close enough to it to enable a dweller to enjoy the Hudson River breezes and the incomparable Hudson River scenery.

Besides, a lot of our friends lived there. There was quite a colony of them scattered over a belt of territory that intervened between the magnificent estates of the multi-millionaires to the southward and the real farming country beyond the Croton Lakes, up the valley. By a process of elimination we had now settled upon the neighborhood where we meant to live. The task of finding a suitable location in this particular area would be an easy one, we thought.

I do not know how the news of this intention spread. We told only a few persons of our purpose. But spread it did, and with miraculous swiftness. Overnight almost, we began to hear from real-estate agents having other people's property to sell and from real-estate owners having their own property to sell. They reached us by mail, by telephone, by messenger, and in person. It was a perfect revelation to learn that so many perfectly situated, perfectly appointed country places, for one reason or another, were to be had for such remarkable figures. Indeed, when we heard the actual amounts the figures were more than remarkable—they were absolutely startling. I am convinced that nothing is so easy to buy as a country place and nothing is so hard to sell. This observation is based upon our own experiences on the buying side and on the experiences of some of my acquaintances who want to sell—and who are taking it out in wanting.

In addition to agents and owners, there came also road builders, well diggers, interior decorators, landscape gardeners, general contractors, an architect or so, agents for nurseries, tree-mending experts, professional foresters, persons desiring to be superintendent of our country place, persons wishful of taking care of our livestock for us—a whole shoal of them. It booted us nothing to explain that we had not yet bought a place; that we had not even looked at a place with the prospect of buying. Almost without exception these callers were willing to sit down with me and use up hours of my time telling me how well qualified they were to deliver the goods as soon as I had bought land, or even before I had bought it.

From the ruck of them as they came avalanching down upon us two or three faces and individualities stand out. There was, for example, the chimney expert. That was what he called himself—a chimney expert. His specialty was constructing chimneys that were guaranteed against smoking, and curing chimneys, built by others, which had contracted the vice. The circumstance of our not having any chimneys of any variety at the moment did not halt him when I had stated that fact to him. He had already removed his hat and overcoat and taken a seat in my study, and he continued to remain right there. He seemed comfortable; in fact, I believe he said he was comfortable.

From chimneys he branched out into a general conversation with me upon the topics of the day.

In my time I have met persons who knew less about a wider range of subjects than he did, but they had superior advantages over him. Some had traveled about over the world, picking up misinformation; some had been educated into a broad and comprehensive ignorance. But here was

Chapter III

a self-taught ignoramus—one, you might say, who had made himself what he was. He may have known all about the habits and shortcomings of flues; but, once you let him out of a chimney, he was adrift on an uncharted sea of mispronounced names, misstated facts and faulty dates.

We discussed the war—or, rather, he erroneously discussed it. We discussed politics and first one thing and then another, until finally the talk worked its way round to literature; and then it was he told me I was one of his favorite authors. "Well," I said to myself, at that, "this person may be shy in some of his departments, but he's all right in others." And then, aloud, I told him that he interested me and asked him to go on.

"Yes, sir," he continued; "I don't care what anybody says, you certainly did write one mighty funny book, anyhow. You've wrote some books that I didn't keer so much for; but this here book, ef it's give me one laugh it's give me a thousand! I can come in dead tired out and pick it up and read a page—yes, read only two or three lines sometimes—and just natchelly bust my sides. How you ever come to think up all them comical sayings I don't, for the life of me, see! I wonder how these other fellers that calls themselves humorists have got the nerve to keep on tryin' to write when they read that book of yours."

"What did you say the name of this particular book was?" I asked, warming to the man in spite of myself.

"It's called Fables in Slang," he said.

I did not undeceive him. He had spoiled my day for me. Why should I spoil his?

Then, there was the persistent nursery-man's agent, with the teeth. He was the most toothsome being I ever saw. The moment he came in, the thought occurred to me that in his youth somebody had put tooth powders into his coffee. He may not have had any more teeth than some people have, but he had a way of presenting his when he smiled or when he spoke, or even when his face was in repose, which gave him the effect of being practically all teeth. Aside from his teeth, the most noticeable thing about him was his persistence.
I began protesting that it would be but a waste of his time and mine to take up the subject of fruit and shade trees and shrubbery, because, even though I might care to invest in his lines, I had at present no soil in which to plant them. But he seemed to regard this as a mere technicality on my part, and before I was anywhere near done with what I meant to say to him he had one arm round me and was filling my lap and my arms and my desk-top with catalogues, price lists, illustrations in color, order slips, and other literature dealing with the products of the house he represented.

I did my feeble best to fight him off; but it was of no use. He just naturally surrounded me. Inside of three minutes he had me as thoroughly mined, flanked and invested as though he'd been Grant and I'd been Richmond. I could tell he was prepared to stay right on until I capitulated.

So, in order for me to be able to live my own life, it became necessary to give him an order. I made it as small an order as possible, because, as I have just said and as I told him repeatedly, I had no place in which to plant the things I bought of him, and could not tell when I should have a place in which to plant them. That petty detail did not concern him in the least. He promised to postpone delivery until I had taken title to some land somewhere; and then he smiled his all-ivory smile and released me from captivity, and took his departure.

Two months later, when we had joined the landed classes, the consignment arrived—peach, pear, quince, cherry and apple. I was quite shocked at the appearance of the various items when we undid the wrappings. The pictures from which I had made my selections showed splendid trees, thick with foliage and laden with the most delicious fruit imaginable. But here, seemingly, was merely a collection of golf clubs in a crude and unfinished state—that is to say, they were about the right length and the right thickness to make golf clubs, but were unfinished to the extent that they had small tentacles or roots adhering to them at their butt ends.

However, our gardener—we had acquired a gardener by then—was of the opinion that they might develop into something. Having advanced this exceedingly sanguine and optimistic belief, he took out a pocket-knife and further maimed the poor little things by pruning off certain minute sprouts or nubs or sprigs that grew upon them; and then he stuck them in the earth. Nevertheless, they grew. At this hour they are still growing, and in time I think they may bear fruit. As a promise of future productivity they bore leaves during the summer—not many leaves, but still enough leaves to keep them from looking so much like walking sticks, and just enough leaves to nourish certain varieties of worms.

I sincerely trust the reader will not think I have been exaggerating in detailing my dealings with the artificers, agents and solicitors who descended upon us when the hue and cry—personally I have never seen a hue, nor, to the best of my knowledge, have I ever heard one; but it is customary to speak of it in connection with a cry and I do so—when, as I say, the presumable hue and the indubitable cry were raised in regard to our ambition to own a country place. Believe me, I am but telling the plain, unvarnished truth. And now we come to the home-seeking enterprise:

Sometimes alone, but more frequently in the company of friends, we toured Westchester, its main highways and its back roads, its nooks and its corners, until we felt that we knew its topography much better than many born and reared in it. Reason totters on her throne when confronted with the task of trying to remember how many places we looked at—places done, places overdone, places underdone, and places undone. Wherever we went, though, one of two baffling situations invariably arose: If we liked a place the price for that place uniformly would be out of our financial reach. If the price were within our reach the place failed to satisfy our desires.

After weeks of questing about, we did almost close for one estate. It was an estate where a rich man, who made his money in town and spent it in the country, had invested a fortune in apple trees. The trees were there—several thousand of them; but they were all such young trees. It would be several years before they would begin to bear, and meantime the services of a small army of men would be required to care for the orchards and prune them, and spray them, and coddle them, and chase insects away from them. I calculated that if we bought this place it would cost me about seven thousand dollars a year for five years ahead in order to enjoy three weeks of pink-and-white beauty in the blossoming time each spring.

Besides, it occurred to me that by the time the trees did begin to bear plentifully the fashionable folk in New York might quit eating apples; in which case everybody else would undoubtedly follow suit and quit eating them too. Ours is a fickle race, as witness the passing of the vogue for iron dogs on front lawns, and for cut-glass vinegar cruets on the dinner table; and a lot of other things, fashionable once but unfashionable now.

Also, the house stood on a bluff directly overlooking the river, with the tracks of the New York Central in plain view and trains constantly ski-hooting by. At the time of our inspection of the premises, long restless strings of freight cars were backing in and out of sidings not more than a quarter of a mile away. We were prepared, after we had moved to the country, to rise with the skylarks, but we could not see the advantage to be derived from rising with the switch engines. Switch engines are notorious for keeping early hours; or possibly the engineers suffer from insomnia.

At length we decided to buy an undeveloped tract and do our own developing. In pursuance of this altered plan we climbed craggy heights with fine views to be had from their crests, but with no water anywhere near; and we waded through marshy meadows, where there was any amount of water but no views. This was discouraging; but we persevered, and eventually perseverance found its reward. Thanks to some kindly souls who guided us to it, we found what we thought we wanted.

We found a sixty-acre tract on a fine road less than a mile and a half from one of the best towns in the lower Hudson Valley. It combined accessibility with privacy; for after you quitted the cleared lands at the front of the property, and entered the woodland at the back, you were instantly in a stretch of timber which by rights belonged in the Adirondacks. About a third of the land was cleared—or, rather, had been cleared once upon a time. The rest was virgin forest running up to the comb of a little mountain, from the top of which you might see, spread out before you and below you, a panorama with a sweep of perhaps forty miles round three sides of the horizon.

There were dells, glades, steep bluffs and rolling stretches of fallow land; there were seven springs on the place; there was a cloven rift in the hill with a fine little valley at the bottom of it, and the first time I clambered up its slope from the bottom I flushed a big cock grouse that went booming away through the underbrush with a noise like a burst of baby thunder. That settled it for me. All my life I have been trying to kill a grouse on the wing, and here was a target right on the premises. Next day we signed the papers and paid over the binder money. We were landowners. Presently we had a deed in the safe-deposit box and some notes in the bank to prove it.

Over most of our friends we had one advantage. They had taken old-fashioned farms and made them over into modern country places. But once upon a time, sixty or seventy years back, the place of which we were now the proud proprietors had been the property of a man of means and good taste, a college professor; and, by the somewhat primitive standards of those days, it had been an estate of considerable pretensions.

This gentleman had done things of which we were now the legatees. For example, he had spared the fine big trees, which grew about the dooryard of his house; and when he had cleared the tillable acres he had left in them here and there little thickets and little rocky copses which stood up like islands from the green expanses of his meadows. The pioneer American farmer's idea of a tree in a field or on a lawn was something that could be cut down right away. Also the original owner had planted orchards of apples and groves of cherries; and he had thrown up stout stone walls, which still stood in fair order.

But—alas!—he had been dead for more than forty years. And during most of those forty years his estate had been in possession of an absentee landlord, a woman, who allowed a squatter to live on the property, rent free, upon one unusual condition—namely, that he repair nothing, change nothing, improve nothing, and, except for the patch where he grew his garden truck, till no land. As well as might be judged by the present conditions, the squatter had lived up to the contract. If a windowpane was smashed he stuffed up the orifice with rags; if a roof broke away he patched the hole with scraps of tarred paper; if a tree fell its moldering trunk stayed where it lay; if brambles sprang up they flourished unvexed by bush hook or pruning blade.

Buried in this wilderness was an old frame residence, slanting tipsily on its rotted sills; and the cellar under it was a noisome damp hole, half filled with stones that had dropped out of the tottering foundation walls. There was a farmer's cottage which from decay and neglect seemed ready to topple over; likewise the remains of a cow barn, where no self-respecting cow would voluntarily spend a night; the moldy ruins of a coach house, an ice house and a chicken house; and flanking these, piles of broken, crumbling boards to mark the sites of sundry cribs and sheds.

The barn alone had resisted neglect and the gnawing tooth of time. This was because it had been built in the time when barns were built to stay. It had big, hand-hewn oak sticks for its beams and rafters and sills; and though its roof was a lacework of rotted shingles and its sides were full of gaps to let the weather in, its frame was as solid and enduring as on the day when it was finished. This, in short and in fine, was what we in our ignorance had acquired. To us it was a splendid asset. Persons who knew more than we did might have called it a liability.

All our friends, though, were most sanguine and most cheerful regarding the prospect. Jauntily and with few words they dismissed the difficulties of the prospect that faced us; and with the same jauntiness we, also, dismissed them.

"Oh, you won't have so very much to do!" I hear them saying. "To be sure, there's a road to be built—not over a quarter of a mile of road, exclusive of the turnround at your garage—when you've built your garage—and the turn in front of your house—when you've built your house. It shouldn't take you long to clear up the fields and get them under cultivation. All you'll have to do there is pick the loose stones off of them and plow the land up, and harrow it and grade it in places, and spread a few hundred wagonloads of fertilizer; and then sow your grass seed. That old horsepond yonder will make you a perfectly lovely swimming pool, once you've cleaned it out and deepened it at this end, and built retaining walls round it, and put in a concrete basin, and waterproofed the sides and bottom. You must have a swimming pool by all means!

"And then, by running a hundred-foot dam across that low place in the valley you can have a wonderful little lake. You surely must have a lake to go with the swimming pool! Then, when you've dug your artesian well, you can couple up all your springs for an emergency supply. You know you can easily pipe the spring water into a tank and conserve it there. Then you'll have all the water you possibly can need—except, of course, in very dry weather in midsummer.

"And, after that, when you've torn the old house down and put up your new house, and built your barn and your stable, and your farmer's cottage and your ice house, and your greenhouses, and your corn-crib, and your tool-shed, and your tennis court, and laid out some terraces up on that hillside yonder, and planned out your flower gardens and your vegetable garden, and your potato patch and your corn patch, and stuck up your chicken runs, and bought your work stock and your cows and chickens and things—oh, yes, and your kennels, if you are going in for dogs—No? All right, then; never mind the kennels. Anyhow, when you've done those things and set out your shrubs and made your rose beds and planted your grapevines, you'll be all ready just to move right in and settle down and enjoy yourselves."

I do not mean that all of these suggestions came at once. As here enumerated they represent the combined fruitage of several conversations on the subject. We listened attentively, making notes of the various notions for our comfort and satisfaction as they occurred to others. If any one had advanced the idea that we should install a private race track, and lay out nine holes, say, of a private golf course, we should have agreed to those items too. These things do sound so easy when you are talking them over and when the first splendid fever of land ownership is upon you!

Had I but known then what I know now! These times, when, going along the road, I pass a manure heap I am filled with envy of the plutocrat who owns it, though, at the same time, deploring the vulgar ostentation that leads him to spread his wealth before the view of the public. When I see a masonry wall along the front of an estate I begin to make mental calculations, for I understand now what that masonry costs, and know that it is cheaper, in the long run, to have your walls erected by a lapidary than by a union stonemason.

And as for a bluestone road—well, you, reader, may think bluestone is but a simple thing and an inexpensive one. Just wait until you have had handed to you the estimates on the cost of killing the nerve and cleaning out the cavities and inserting the fillings, and putting in the falsework and the bridgework, and the drains and the arches—and all! You might think dentists are well paid for such jobs; but a professional road contractor—I started to say road agent—makes any dentist look a perfect piker.

And any time you feel you really must have a swimming pool that is all your very own, take my advice and think twice. Think oftener than twice; and then compromise on a neat little outdoor sitz bath that is all your very own.

But the inner knowledge of these things was to come to us later. For the time being, pending the letting of contracts, we were content to enjoy the two most pleasurable sensations mortals may know—possession and anticipation: the sense of the reality of present ownership and, coupled with this, dreams of future creation and future achievement. We were on the verge of making come true the treasured vision of months—we were about to become abandoned farmers.

No being who is blessed with imagination can have any finer joy than this, I think—the joy of proprietorship of a strip of the green footstool. The soil you kick up when you walk over your acres is different soil from that which you kick up on your neighbor's land—different because it is yours. Another man's tree, another man's rock heap, is a simple tree or a mere rock heap, as the case may be; and nothing more. But your tree and your rock heap assume a peculiar value, a special interest, a unique and individual picturesqueness.

And oh, the thrill that permeates your being when you see the first furrow of brown earth turned up in your field, or the first shovel-load of sod lifted from the spot where your home is to stand! And oh, the first walk through the budding woods in the springtime! And the first spray of trailing arbutus! And the first spray of trailing poison ivy! And the first mortgage! And the first time you tread on one of those large slick brown worms, designed, inside and out, like a chocolate éclair!

After all, it's the only life! But on the way to it there are pitfalls and obstacles and setbacks, and steadily mounting monthly pay rolls.

As shall presently develop.

IV

Happy Days for Major Gloom

Soon after we moved to the country we became eligible to join the Westchester County Despair Association, on account of an artesian well—or, to be exact, on account of three artesian wells, complicated with several springs.

I spoke some pages back of the Westchester County Despair Association, which was founded by George Creel and which has a large membership in our immediate section. As I stated then, any city-bred man who turns amateur farmer and moves into our neighborhood, and who in developing his country place has a streak of hard labor, is eligible to join this organization. And sooner or later—but as a general thing sooner—all the urbanites who settle up our way do join. Some day we shall be strong enough to club in and elect our own county officers on a ticket pledged to run a macadam highway past the estate of each member.

Our main claim to qualification was based upon the water question; and yet at the outset it appeared to us that lack of water would be the very least of our troubles. When we took title to our abandoned farm, and for the first time explored the bramble-grown valley leading up from the proposed site of our house to the woodland, we several times had to wade, and once or twice thought we should have to swim. Why, we actually congratulated ourselves upon having acquired riparian rights without paying for them.

This was in the springtime; and the springs along the haunches of the hills upon either side of the little ravine were speaking in burbly murmuring voices, like overflowing mouths, as they spilled forth their accumulated store of the melted snows of the winter before; and the April rainstorms had made a pond of every low place in the county.

In our ignorance we assumed that, since there was now plenty of water of Nature's furnishing, there always would be plenty of water forthcoming from the same prodigal source—more water than we could possibly ever need unless we opened up a fresh-water bathing beach in the lower meadow of our place. So we dug out and stoned up the uppermost spring, which seemed to have the most generous vein of them all, and put in pipes. The lay of the land and the laws of gravity did the rest, bringing the flow downgrade in a gurgling comforting stream, which poured day and night without cessation.

This detail having been attended to, we turned our attention to other things. Goodness knows there were plenty of things requiring attention. I figured at that period of our pioneering work that if we got into the Despair Association at all it would follow as the result of my being indicted for more or less justifiable manslaughter in having destroyed an elderly gentleman of the vicinity, whom upon the occasion of our first meeting I rechristened as Old Major Gloom, and of whom we still speak behind his back by that same name.

The major lived a short distance from us, within easy walking distance, and he speedily proved that he was an easy walker. I shall not forget the first day he came to call. He ambled up a trail that the previous tenants, through a chronic delusion, had insisted upon calling a road; and he found me up to my gills in the midst of the preliminary job of trying to decide where we should make a start at clearing out the jungle, which once upon a time, probably back in the Stone Age, as nearly as we might judge from its present condition, had been the house garden.

We had been camping on the place only a few days. We climbed over, through and under mystic mazes of household belongings to get our meals, or to get to our beds, or to get anywhere, and altogether were existing in a state of disorder that might be likened to the condition the Germans created with such thoroughgoing and painstaking efficiency when falling back from an occupied French community.

I trust we are not lacking in hospitality; but, for the moment, we were in no mood to receive visitors. However, upon first judgment the old major's appearance was such as to disarm hostility and re-arouse the slumbering instincts of cordiality. He was of a benevolent aspect, with fine white whiskers and an engaging manner. If you can imagine one of the Minor Prophets, who had stepped right out of the Old Testament, stopping en route at a ready-made clothing store, you will have a very fair mental picture of the major as he looked when he approached me, with hand outstretched, and in warm tones bade me welcome to Upper Westchester. He fooled me; he would have fooled anybody unless possibly it were an expert criminologist, trained at discerning depravity when masked behind a pleasing exterior.

When he spoke I placed him with regard to his antecedents, for I had been on the spot long enough to recognize the breed to which he belonged. There is a type of native-born citizen of this part of New York State who

Happy Days for Major Gloom

comes of an undiluted New England strain, being the descendant of pioneering Yankees who settled along the lower Hudson Valley after the Revolution and immediately started in to trade the original Dutch settlers out of their lands and their eyeteeth.

The subsequent generations of this transplanted stock have preserved some of the customs and many of the idioms of their stern and rock-bound forebears; at the same time they have acquired most of the linguistic eccentricities of the New York cockney. Except that they dwell in proximity to it, they have nothing in common with the great city that is only thirty or forty miles away as the motorist flies. Generally they profess a contempt for New York and all its works. They may not visit it once a year; but, all the same, its influence has crept up through the hills to tincture their mode of speech with queer distinctive modes of pronunciation.

The result is a composite dialectic system not to be found anywhere else except in this little strip of upland country and in certain isolated communities over on Long Island, along the outer edge of the zone of metropolitan life and excitement. For instance, a member of this race of beings will call a raspberry a "rosbry"; and he will call a bluebird a "blubbud," thereby displaying the inherited vernacular of the Down East country. He will say "oily" when he means early, and "early" when he means oily, and occasionally he will even say "yous" for you—peculiarities which in other environment serve unmistakably to mark the born-and-bred Manhattanite.

The major at once betrayed himself as such a person. He introduced himself, adding that as a neighbor he had felt it incumbent to call. I removed a couple of the family portraits and a collection of Indian relics and a few kitchen utensils, and one thing and another, from the seat of a chair, and begged him to sit down and make himself at home, which he did. He accepted a cigar, which I fished out of a humidor temporarily tucked away beneath a roll of carpet; and we spoke of the weather, to which he gave a qualified and cautious indorsement. Then, without further delay, he hitched his chair over and laid a paternal hand upon my arm.

"I hear you've got Blank, the lawyer, searching out the title to your propputty here."

"Yes," I said; "Mr. Blank took the matter in hand for us. Fine man, isn't he?"

"Well, some people think so," he said with an emphasis of profound significance.

"Doesn't everybody think so?" I inquired.

"Listen," he said; "my motto is, Live and let live. And, anyhow, I'm the last man in the world to go round prejudicing a newcomer against an old resident. Now I've just met you and, on the other hand, I've known Blank all my life; in fact, we're sort of related by marriage—a relative of his married a relative of my wife's. So, of course, I've got nothing to say to you on that score except this—and I'm going to say it to you now in the strictest confidence—if I was doing business with Blank I'd be mighty, mighty careful, young man."

"You astonish me," I said. "Mr. So-and-So"—naming a prominent business man of the county seat—"recommended his firm to me."

"Oh, So-and-So, eh? I wonder what the understanding between those two is? Probably they've hatched up something."

"Why, isn't So-and-So above suspicion?" I asked.

"I wouldn't say he was and I wouldn't say he wasn't. But, just between you and me, I'd think twice about taking any advice he gave me. They tell me you've let the contract for some work to Dash & Space?"

"Yes; I gave them one small job."

"Too bad!"

"What's too bad?"

"You'll be finding out for yourself before you're done; so I won't say anything more on that subject neither. I could tell you a good deal about those fellows if I was a-mind to; but I never believed in repeating anything behind a man's back I wouldn't say to his face. Live and let live!—that's my motto. Anyhow, if you've already signed up with Dash & Space it's too late for you to be backing out—but keep your eyes open, young man; keep your eyes wide open. Who's your architect going to be?"

I told him. He repeated the name in rather a disappointed fashion.

"Never heard of him," he admitted; "but I take it he's like the run of his kind of people. I never yet saw the architect that I'd trust as far as I could sling him by the coat-tails. Say, ain't that Bink's delivery wagon standing over yonder in front of your stable?"

"I think so. We've been buying some things from Bink."

"You've opened up a regular account with him, then?"

"Yes."

"Well, I wouldn't reflect on Bink's honesty for any amount of money in the world. Of my own knowledge I don't know anything against him one way or the other. Of course, from time to time I've heard a lot of things that other people said about him; but that's only hearsay evidence, and I make it a rule not to repeat gossip about anybody. Still"—he lingered over the word—"still, if it was me instead of you, I'd go over his bills very carefully—that's all!

"I don't blame any fellow for trying to get along in his business; and I guess the competition is so keen in the retail merchandising line that once in a while a man just naturally has to skin his customers a little. But that's no argument why he should try to take the entire hide off of 'em. They tell me Bink's bookkeeper is a regular wizard when it comes to making up an account, 'specially for a stranger." He took a puff or two at his cigar, meantime squinting across our weed-grown fields. "Don't I see 'Lonzo Begee chopping dead trees down there alongside the road?"

"Yes; I believe that's his name. He only came to work for us this morning. Seems to be a hustler."

"Does he, now? Well, ain't it a curious circumstance how many fellers starting in at a new job just naturally work their heads off and wind up at the end of the second week loafing? Strikes me that's particularly the case with the farm laborers round here. Now you take 'Lonzo Begee's case. He never worked for me—I'm mighty careful about who I hire, lemme tell you!—but it always struck me as a strange thing that 'Lonzo changes jobs so often. I make it a point to keep an eye on what's happening in this neighborhood; and seems like every time I run acrost him he's working in a different place for a different party.

"And yet you never can tell—he might turn out to be a satisfactory hand for you. Stranger things have happened. And besides, what suits one man don't suit another. I believe in letting a man find out about these things for himself. The bitterer the experience and the more it costs him, the more likely he is to remember the lesson and profit by it. Don't you think so yourself?"

I told him I thought so; and presently he took his departure, after remarking that we had purchased a place with a good many possibilities in it; though, from what he had heard, we probably paid too much for it, and he only hoped we didn't waste too much money in developing. He left me filled with so many doubts and so many misgivings that I felt congested. Within two days he was back, though, still actuated by the neighborly spirit, to warn me against a few more persons with whom we had already had dealings, or with whom we expected to have dealings, or with whom conceivably we might some day have dealings.

And within a week after that he returned a third time to put me on my guard against one or two more individuals who somehow had been overlooked by him in his previous visits. Rarely did he come out in the open and accuse anybody of anything. He was too crafty, too subtle for that. The major was a regular sutler. But he certainly did understand the art of planting the poison. Give him time enough, and he could destroy a fellow's confidence in the entire human race.

He specialized in no single direction; his gifts were ample for all emergencies. When he tired of making you distrustful of those about you, or when temporarily he ran out of material, he knew the knack of making you distrustful of your own judgment. For example, there was the time, in the second month of our acquaintance I think it was, when he meandered in to inspect the work of renovation that had just been started on the stable. He spent perhaps ten minutes going over the premises, now and then uttering low, disparaging, clucking sounds under his breath. I followed him about fearsomely. I was distressed on account of the disclosures that I felt would presently be forthcoming.

"Putting on a slate roof, eh?" he said when he was done with the investigation. "Expect it to stay put?"

I admitted that such had been the calculation of the builder.

"Nothing like being one of these here optimists," he commented dryly. "But I want to tell you that it's the biggest mistake you ever made to put a slate roof on those sloping gables without sticking in some metal uprights to keep the snow from sliding off in a lump when the winter thaws come."

It had always seemed to me that snow had few enough pleasures as it was. Though I had given the subject but little thought, it appeared to me that if sliding off a roof gave the snow any satisfaction it would ill become me or any one else to interfere. I ventured to say as much.

"I guess you don't get my meaning," he explained. "When the snow starts sliding, if there's enough of it, it's purty sure to take most of those slates along with it. And then where'll you be, I want to know?"

"Is—is it too late to put up some anti-sliding thingumbobs now?" I asked.

"Oh, yes," he said comfortingly; "it's too late now unless you ripped the whole job off and started all over again. I judge you'll just have to let Nature take its course. I see you've got a chimney that don't come over the ridge of the roof. Are you calculating that it'll draw?"

"I rather hoped it would—that was the intention, I believe."

"Well, then, you're in for another disappointment there. But if I was you I shouldn't fret myself about that, because it'll be some months yet before you'll be building a fire in the fireplace, what with the warm weather just coming on; and you can have the top of the chimney lifted almost any time.... I don't want to alarm you needlessly; but it looks to me like mighty faulty drainpipes the plumber's been putting in for you. You'll have to snatch all that out before a great while and have new pipes put in proper. Don't it beat all what sharpers plumbers are? But then, they're no worse than other artisans, taking them by and large. F'r instance, what could be a worse job than that plastering in your bedroom, or those tin gutters up yonder at your eaves? The plastering may stay up a while, but the first good hard storm ought to bring the gutters down. I don't like your masonry work, either, if you're asking me for my opinion; and I see the carpenters are slipping in some mighty sorry-looking flooring on you."

I am not exaggerating. I am repeating, as accurately as I can, a conversation that really took place.

For a while the major was in a fair way to spoil the present century for me. If the inhabitants of the countryside were in a conspiracy to strip the pelfry off a fresh arrival and divide it among them as souvenirs, if there was no honesty left anywhere in a corrupted world, what, then, was the use of living? Why not commit suicide according to one of the standard methods and have done with the struggle, trusting that the undertaker would not be too much of a gouge and that the executors of the estate would leave a trifle of it for the widow and the orphan?

But, after a spell, during which from the various firms, corporations and persons who had been traduced by him we uniformly had considerate and fair and scrupulously honorable treatment and service, we began to disregard the major's danger signals and to steer right past them. He, though, wearied not in well-doing. At every chance he dropped in, a poison viper disguised as a philanthropist, to hang another red light on the switch for us. It was inevitable that his ministrations should get on our nerves. I began to have visions centering about justifiable acts of homicide, always with the major for the chosen victim of my violence.

It was after having such a dream that I figured myself as getting into George Creel's Despair Association by virtue of having to stand trial over at White Plains for murder. As a matter of fact, I spared the major; and at last accounts he was still going to and fro in the land, planting slanders on all likely sites. I take it that there is one counterpart for him among every so many human beings; but it is in the country where every one has a chance to find out every one's business, and where the excuses of being neighborly and friendly give him opportunity for plying his trade that he is most in evidence.

V

In Which We Bore for Water

    We joined the Despair Association finally by reason of our water problem. However, that was to come into our lives later. Through the springtime we had more water than we could possibly hope to use, and we focused our attentions and our energies upon hacking a homestead out of the briar patch we had bought.

    A painful acre at a time, we cleared lands that once had been cleared. As I may have stated already, forty-odd years of disuse had turned lawn space, garden space and meadow into one conglomerate jungle of towering weeds and tangled thorny underbrush, stretching from the broken fences along the highroad straight back to the dooryard of the moldering tumbledown dwelling. With a gang of men under a competent foreman, and a double team of hired horses, we assaulted that tangle, bringing to the undertaking much of the same ardor and some of the same fortitude which I imagine must have inspired Stanley on the day when he began chopping his way through the trackless wilds of the dark forest to find Doctor Livingstone.

It gave one the feeling of being a pioneer and a pathfinder—no, not a pathfinder; a pathmaker—to stand by, superintending in a large, broad, general, perfectly ignorant fashion the job of opening up those thickets of ours to the sunlight that had not visited them for ever so long. Off of one segment of our property, a slope directly behind the main house, we took over four hundred wagonloads of stumps, roots, trunks, boughs and brush—the fruitage of nearly two months of steady labor on the part of men and horses.

The brambles were shorn down and piled in heaps to be burned. The locusts, thousands of them, varying in size from half-grown trees to switchy saplings, were by main force snatched out of the ground bodily. A number of long-dead chestnuts and hickories, great unsightly snags that reared above the uptorn harried earth like monuments to past neglect, were felled and sawed into cordwood lengths and carted away.

In Which We Bore for Water

What emerged after these things had been done more than repaid us for all our pains. When the rumpled soil had been smoothed back and plowed and harrowed, and sown to grass, and when the grass had sprouted as promptly as it did, there stood forth a dimpling green expanse where before had been a damp, moldy and almost impenetrable tangle, hiding treasure-troves of old tin cans, heaps of rusted and broken farming implements and here and there the bleached-out bones of a dead cow or a deceased horse.

To our abounding astonishment, we found ourselves the owners of a considerable number of old but healthy apple trees and a whole grove of cherry trees that we hadn't known were there at all, so thoroughly had they been buried in the locusts and the sumacs. It was just like finding them. Indeed, it was finding them.

The old house came down next, with some slight assistance from a crew of wreckers. Being almost ready to come down of its own accord it met them halfway. They had merely to pry into the foundations, hit her a hard wallop in the ribs, and then run for their lives. From the wreckage we reclaimed, out of the cellar, which was pre-Revolutionary, some hand-hewn oak beams in a perfect state of preservation; and out of the upper floors, which were pre-James K. Polk, a quantity of interior trim, along with door frames and window sashes.

Incidentally we dispossessed a large colony of rats and a whole synod of bats, a parish of yellow wasps and a small but active congregation of dissenting cats—half-wild, glary-eyed, roach-backed, mangy cats that resided under the broken flooring. In all there were fourteen of these cats—swift and rangy performers, all of them. One and all, they objected to being driven from home. They hung about the razed wreckage, and by night they convened in due form upon a bare knoll hard by, and held indignation meetings.

Parliamentary disputes arose frequently, with the result that the proceedings might be heard for a considerable distance. I took steps to break up these deliberations, and after several of the principal debaters had met a sudden end—I am a very good wing shot on cats—the survivors saw their way clear to departing entirely from the vicinity. Within a week thereafter the song birds, which until then had been strangely scarce upon the premises, heard the news, and began coming in swarms. We put up nesting boxes and feeding shelves, and long before June arrived we had hundreds of feathered boarders and a good many pairs of feathered tenants.

One morning in the early part of the month of June I counted within sight at one time fourteen varieties of birds, including such brilliantly colored specimens as a scarlet tanager and his mate; a Baltimore oriole; a bluebird; an indigo bunting; a chat; and a flicker—called, where I came from, a yellow hammer. Robins were probing for worms in the rank grass; two brown thrashers and a black-billed cuckoo were investigating the residential possibilities of a cedar tree not far away; and from the woods beyond came the sound of a cock grouse drumming his amorous fanfare on a log.

Think of what that meant to a man who, for the better part of twelve years, had been hived up in a flat, with English sparrows for company, when he craved a bit of wild life!

What had been a gardener's cottage stood at the roadside a hundred yards away from the site of the main house. On first examination it seemed fit only for the scrap heap; but one of those wise elderly persons who are to be found in nearly every rural community—a genius who was part carpenter, part mason, part painter, part glazier and part plasterer—was called into consultation, and he decided that, given time and material for mending, he might be able to do something with the shell. Modestly he called himself an odd-jobs man; really he was a doctor to decrepit and ailing structures.

From neglect and dry rot the patient was almost gone; but he nursed it back to a new lease on life, trepanning its top with new rafters, splinting its broken sides with new clapboards. He cured the cellar walls of rickets, the roof of baldness, and the inside woodwork of tetter; and he so wrought with hammer and saw and nails, with lime and cement, with paintbrush and putty knife, that presently what had been a most disreputable blot on the landscape became not only a livable little house but an exceedingly picturesque one, what with its wide overhanging gables, its cocky little front veranda, and its new complexion of roughcast stucco.

While this transformation was accomplished in the lower field, we were doing things to the barn up on the hillside. It had good square lines, the barn had; and, though its outer casing was in a woeful state of nonrepair, its frame, having been built sixty or seventy years ago of splendid big timbers, stood straight and unskewed. Thanks to the ability of our architect to dream an artistic dream and then to create it, this structure, without impairment of its general lines and with no change at all in its general dimensions, presently became a combination garage and bungalow.

The garage part was down below, occupying the space formerly given over to horse stalls and cow sheds. Here, also, a furnace room, a laundry and a servant's room were built in. Above were the housekeeping quarters—three bedrooms; two baths; a big living hall, with a wide-mouthed fireplace in it; a kitchen, and a pantry. This floor had been the haymow; but I'll warrant that if any of the long-vanished hay which once rested there could have returned it wouldn't have known the old place.

The roof of the transmogrified mow was sufficiently high to permit the construction of a roomy attic, with accommodations for one sleeper at one end of it, and ample storage space besides.

At the back of the building, where the teams had driven in, a little square courtyard of weathered brick was laid; a roof of rough Vermont slate was laid on in an irregular splotchy pattern of buff and yellow and black squares; and finally, upon the front, at the level of the second floor, the builder hung on a little Italian balcony, from which on clear days, looking south down the Hudson, we have a forty-mile stretch of landscape and waterscape before us.

On the nearer bank, two miles away, the spires of the market town show above the tree tops; on the further bank, six miles away, the rumpled blue outlines of the Ramapo Hills bulk up against the sky line; and back of those hills are sunsets such as ambitious artists try, more or less unsuccessfully, to put on canvas.

All this had not cost so much as it might have, because all the interior trim, all the doors and windows, and all the studs and joists and beams had been reclaimed from the demolished main building. The chief extravagances had been a facing of stonework for the garage front and a stucco dress for the upper walls. We broke camp and moved in.

For a month or so we went along swimmingly. One morning we quit swimming. All of a sudden we woke up to find there was no longer sufficient water for aquatic pastimes.

The absolutely unprecedented dry spell that occurs every second or third year in this part of the North Temperate Zone had descended upon us, taking us, as it were, unawares. The brooks were going dry; the grass on hillsides where the soil was thin turned from a luscious green to a parched brown; and the mother spring of our seven up the valley, which had gushed so plenteously, now diminished overnight, as it were, into a puny runlet. There were no indications that the spring would be absolutely dry; but there was every indication that it would continue to lessen in the volume of its output—which it did. We summoned friends and well-wishers into consultation, and by them were advised to dig an artesian well.

We did not want to bother with artesian wells then. We were living very comfortably upstairs over the garage and we were planning the house we meant to build. We had drawn plans, and yet more plans, torn them up and started all over again; and had found doing this to be one of the deepest pleasures of life. Time without end we had conferred with friends who had built houses of their own, and who gave us their ideas of the things which would be absolutely indispensable to our comfort and happiness in our new house. We had incorporated these ideas with a few of our own, and then we had found that if we meant to construct a house which would please all concerned, ourselves included, there would be needed a bond issue to float the enterprise and the completed structure would be about the size of a cathedral. So then we would trim down, paring off a breakfast porch here and a conservatory there, until we had a design for a compact edifice not much larger than an average-sized railroad terminal.

In Which We Bore for Water

Between times, when not engaged in the pleasing occupation of building our house on paper, we chose the site where it should stand. This, also, consumed a good many days, because each time we decided on a different location. One of our favorite recreations was shifting the house we meant to build about from place to place. We put imaginary wheels under that imaginary home of ours and kept it traveling all over the farm. The trouble with us was we had too much latitude. With half an acre of land at our disposal, we should have been circumscribed by boundary lines. On half an acre you have to be reasonably definite about where you are going to build; slide too far one way or the other, and you are committing trespass, and litigation ensues. But we had sixty acres from which to pick and to choose—sixty acres, with desirable sites scattered all over the tract.

No sooner had we absolutely and positively settled on one spot as the spot where the house must stand than we would find half a dozen others equally desirable, or even more so; and then, figuratively speaking, we would pick up the establishment and transport it to one of the newly discovered spots, and wheel it round to face in a different direction from the direction in which it had just been facing. If a thing that does not yet physically exist may have sensations, the poor dizzy thing must have felt as if it were a merry-go-round.

Likewise we were very busy putting in our road. Up until a short time ago Miss Anna Peck, who makes a specialty of scaling supposedly inaccessible crags, was probably the only living person who could have derived any pleasure from penetrating to our mountain fastness, either afoot or otherwise. When we heard an engine in difficulties coughing down under the hill, followed by the sound of a tire blowing out, or by the smell of rubber scorching as the brakes clamped into the fabric, we knew some of our friends had been reckless enough to undertake to climb up by motor. So, unless we wanted to become hermits, we felt it incumbent upon us to put in a road.

When we got the estimates on the job we decided that the contractor must have figured on building our road of chalcedony or onyx or moss agate or some other of the semi-precious stones. It didn't seem possible that he meant to use any native material—at that price. It turned out, though, that his bid was fairly moderate—as processed bluestone roads go in this climate; and ours has cost us only about eight times as much as I had previously supposed a replica of the Appian Way would cost. However, it has been pronounced a very good road by critics who should know; not a fancy road, but a fair average one.

It would look smarter, of course, with wide brick gutters down either side of it for its entire length; and I should add brick gutters, too, if I were as comfortably fixed, say, as Mr. Charles Schwab, and felt sure that I could get some of the Vanderbilt boys to help me out in case I ran short of funds before the job was completed. Still, for persons who live simply it does very well.

With all these absorbing employments to engage us, we naturally were loath to turn our attentions to water. We had lived too long in a flat where, when you wanted water, you merely turned a faucet. To us water had always been a matter of course. But now the situation was different. With each succeeding day the flow from our spring was slackening. In its present puniness it was no more than a reminder of the brave stream of the springtime.

There was a water witch, so called, in the neighborhood—a gentleman water witch. We were recommended to avail ourselves of his services. It was his custom, we were told, to arm himself with a forked peach-tree switch and walk about over the land, holding the wand in front of him by its two prongs, meantime muttering strange incantations. When he came to a spot where water lay close to the surface the other end of his divining rod would dip magically toward the earth. You dug there, and if you struck water the magician took the credit for it; and if you didn't strike water it was a sign the peach-tree switch had wilfully deceived its proprietor, and he cut a fresh twig off another and more dependable tree and gave you a second demonstration at half rates. However, before opening negotiations with this person, I bethought me to interview the man who had contracted to do the boring.

The latter gentleman proved to be the most noncommittal man I ever met in my life. He was as chary about making predictions as to the result of operations in his line as the ticket agent of a jerkwater railroad down South is about estimating the probable time of arrival of the next passenger train—always conceding that there is to be any next train; and that is as chary as any human being can possibly be. Only upon one thing was he positive, which was that no peach-tree switch in the world could be educated up to the point where it could find water that was hidden underground.

Man and boy, he had been boring wells for thirty years, he said; and it was all guess. One shaft would be put down—at three dollars a foot—until it pierced the roof of Tophet, and the only resultant moisture would be night sweats for the unhappy party who was footing the bills. Or the same prospector might dig his estate so full of circular holes that it would resemble honeycomb tripe, and never get anything except monthly statements for the work to date. On the other hand, a luckier man, living right across the way, had been known to start sinking a shaft, and before the drill had gone twenty feet it became necessary to remove the women and children to a place of safety until the geyser had been throttled down.

This particular well digger's business, as he himself explained, was digging wells, not filling them after they were dug. He guaranteed to make a hole in the ground of suitable caliber for an artesian well, but Nature and Providence must do the rest. With this understanding, he fetched up his outfit and greased himself and the machinery all over, and announced that he was ready to start.

So we picked out a spot where it would be convenient to build a pump house afterward, and he fixed up the engine and began grinding away. And he ground and ground and ground. Every morning, whistling a cheerful air, he would set his drills in circular motion, and all day he would keep it turning and turning. At eventide I would call on him and he would report progress—he had advanced so many feet or so many yards in a southerly direction and had encountered such and such a formation.

"Any water?" At first I would put up the question hopefully, then nervously, and finally for the sake of regularity merely.

"No water," he would reply blithely; "but this afternoon about three o'clock I hit a stratum of the prettiest white quartz you ever saw in your life."

And, with the passion of the born geologist gleaming in his eye, he would pick up a handful of shining specimens and hold them out for me to admire; but I am afraid that toward the last any enthusiasm displayed by me was more or less forced.

And the next night it would be red sandstone, or gray mica, or sky-blue schist, or mottled granite, or pink iron ore—or something! This abandoned farm of ours certainly proved herself to be a mighty variegated mineral prospect. In the course of four weeks that six-inch hole brought forth silver and solder, soda and sulphur, borax and soapstone, crystal and gravel, amalgam fillings and a very fair grade of moth balls.

It brought forth nearly everything that may be found beneath the surface of the earth, I think, except radium—and water. On second thought, I am not so sure about the radium. It occurs to me that we did strike a trace of something resembling radium at the two-hundred-foot level—I won't be positive. But I am absolutely sure about the water. There wasn't any.

At the end of a long and expensive month we abandoned that hole, fruitful though it was in mineral wealth, moved the machinery a hundred yards west, and began all over again. We didn't get any water here, either; but before we quit we ran into a layer of wonderful white marble. If anybody ever discovers a way of getting marble for monuments and statuary out of a hole six inches in diameter and a hundred and seventy-five feet deep our fortunes are made. We have the hole and the marble at the bottom of it; all he will have to provide is the machinery.

By now we were desperate, but determined. We sent word to George Creel to rush us application blanks for membership in his Despair Association. We transferred the digging apparatus to a point away down in the valley, and the contractor retuned his engine and inserted a new steel

In Which We Bore for Water

drill—his other one had been worn completely out—and we began boring a third time. And three weeks later—oh, frabjous joy!—we struck water—plenteous oodles of it; cold, clear and pure. And then we broke ground for our new house.

That isn't all—by no means is it all. Free from blight, our potatoes are in the bin; our apples have been picked; and our corn has been gathered, and in a rich golden store, it fills our new corncrib. We are eating our own chickens and our own eggs; we are drinking milk from our own cow; and we are living on vegetables of our own raising.

Until now I never cared deeply for turnips. Turnips, whether yellow or white, meant little in my life. But now I know that was because they were strange turnips, not turnips which had grown in our own soil and for which I could have almost a paternal affection. Last night for dinner I ate a derby hatful of mashed turnips, size seven and an eighth.

Let the servants quit now if they will—and do. Only the day before yesterday the laundress walked out on us. It was our new laundress, who had succeeded the old laundress, the one who stayed with us for nearly two consecutive weeks before the country life palled upon her sensitive spirit. And the day before that we lost a perfect treasure of a housemaid. She disliked something that was said by some one occupying the comparatively unimportant position of a member of the family, and she took umbrage and some silverware and departed from our fireside. We've had our troubles with cooks, too.

When the latest one showed signs of a gnawing discontent I offered to take lessons on the ukulele and play for her in the long winter evenings that are now upon us. I suggested that we think up charades and acrostics—I am very fertile at acrostics—and have anagram parties now and then to while away the laggard hours. But no; she felt the call of the city and she must go. We are expecting a fresh candidate to-morrow. We shall try to make her stay with us, however brief, a pleasant one.

But these domestic upsets are to us as nothing at all; for we have struck water, and we are living, in part at least, on our own home-grown provender, and shortly we shall start the home of our dreams. And to-day something else happened that filled our cup of joy to overflowing. In the middle of the day a dainty little doe came mincing down through our garden just as confidently as though she owned the place.

We are less than an hour by rail from the Grand Central Station; and yet, as I write this line, a lordly cock grouse is strutting proud and unafraid through the undergrowth not fifty yards from my workroom! Last night, when I opened my bedroom window—in the garage—to watch the distant reflection of the New York lights, flickering against the sky to the southward, I heard a dog fox yelping in the woods!

Let Old Major Gloom, the human Dismal Swamp, come over now as often as pleases him. Our chalice is proof against his poison.

VI

Two More Years Elapse

As the reader will have no trouble in recalling, we broke ground for our house. That, however, was after we had altered the design so often that the first lot of plans and specifications got vertigo and had to be retired in favor of a new set. For one thing, we snatched one entire floor out of the original design—just naturally jerked it out from under and cast it away and never missed it either. And likewise this was after we had shifted the site of the house from one spot to another spot and thence to a third likely spot, and finally back again to the first spot. This, however, had one thing in its favor at least. It enabled us to do our moving without taking our household goods from storage, and yet during the same period to enjoy all the pleasurable thrill of shifting about from place to place. I find moving in your mind is a much less expensive way than the other way is and gives almost as much pleasure to a woman, who—being a woman—is naturally a mover at heart.

Finally, though, all this preliminary skirmishing came to an end and we actually started work on our house. I should say, we started work on what formerly we had thought was going to be our house. It turned out we were wrong. As it stands to-day, two years after the beginning, in a state approaching completion, it is a very satisfactory sort of house we think, artistically as well as from the standpoint of being practical and comfortable; but it is no longer entirely our house. The architect is responsible for the general scheme of things, for the layout and the assembling of the wood and the brick and the cement and the stonework and all that sort of thing, and to him largely will attach the credit if the effect within and without should prove pleasing to the eye. Likewise, here and there are to be found the traces of ideas which we ourselves had, but I must confess the structure is also a symposium of the modified ideas of our friends and well-wishers mated to our ideas.

To me human nature presents a subject for constant study. For a thing so widely distributed as it is, I regard it as one of the most interesting things there are anywhere. It seems to me one of the chief peculiarities of human nature is that it divides all civilized mankind into two special groups—those who think they could run any newspaper better than the man who is trying to run it, and those who think they could run any hotel better than the man who is hanging on as manager or proprietor of it. There are subdivisional classifications of course—for example, women who think they can tell any other woman how to bring up her children without spoiling them to death, and women who are absolutely sure no woman on earth can tell them anything about the right way to bring up their own children; which two groupings include practically all women. And I have yet to meet the man who did not believe that he was a good judge of either horses, diamonds, wines, women, salad dressings, antique furniture, Oriental rugs or the value of real estate. And finally all of these, regardless of sex and regardless, too, of previous experience in the line, know better how a house intended for living purposes should be designed and arranged than the individuals who are paying the bills and who expect to tenant the house as a home when it is done. By the same token—or by the inverse ratio of the same token—the persons who are building the house invariably begin to have doubts and misgivings regarding the worth of their own pet notions in regard to the said house the moment some outsider offers a counter argument. I do not know why this last should be so, but it is. It merely is one of the inexplicable phases of the common phenomenon called human nature.

In our own case the force of this fact applied with a pronounced emphasis. When the tentative draft of the house of our dreams was offered for our inspection it seemed to us a gem—perfect, precious and rare. Filled with pride as we were, we showed the drawings to every one who came to see us. Getting out the drawings when somebody called became a regular habit with us. Being ourselves so deeply interested in them, we couldn't understand why our friends shouldn't be interested too. And they were—I'll say that much for them; they were all interested. And why not? For one thing, it gave them a chance to show how right they were regarding the designing of a house; not our house particularly, but anything under a roof, ranging from St. Peter's at Rome to the façade of the government fish hatchery in Tupelo, Mississippi. For another thing, it gave them a chance to show us how completely wrong we were on this subject. Not a single soul among them but pounced at the opportunity. Until then I never realized how many born pouncers—not amateur pouncers but professional expert master pouncers—I numbered in my acquaintance. Right from the beginning the procedure followed a certain ritual. A caller or pouncer would drop in and have off his things and get comfortably settled. We would produce the sketches, fondling them lovingly, and spread them out and invite the attention of our guest to probably the only perfect design of a house fashioned by the mind of man since the days of the mound builders on this hemisphere. In our language we may not have gone quite so far as to say all this, but our manner indicated that such was the case.

He—for convenience in the illustration I shall make him a man, though in the case of a woman the outcome remained the same—he would consider the matchless work of inventive art presented for his consideration and then he would say:

"An awfully nice notion—splendid, perfectly splendid! And still, you know, if I were—" And so on.

Or perhaps it would be: "Oh, I like the general idea immensely! But—you'll pardon my making a little suggestion, won't you?—but if I were tackling this proposition—" And so on.

It has been my observation that all complimentary remarks uttered by a member of the human race in connection with a house which somebody else contemplates building end in "but."

You just simply can't get away from it.

From the treasure-troves of my memory I continue to quote:

"But if I were tackling this proposition I would certainly not put the dining room here where you've got it. I'd switch it over there right next to the living room and give a vista through. See, like this!"

And out would come his lead pencil.

"But that would mean eliminating the main hall," one of us would venture.

"Of course it would," Brother Pounce would say. "Next to giving a vista through, cutting out the hall is the principal idea I had in mind. What do you want with a hall here? For that matter, what do you want with a hall any place that you can get along without it? Why, my dear people, don't you know that hallways are no earthly good except to catch dust and be drafty and make extra work for servants? And besides, in modern houses people are cutting the hallways down to a minimum—to an absolute minimum."

We gathered that in a modern house—and, of course, a modern house was what we devoutly craved to own—persons going from one part of it to another didn't pass through a hall any more; they passed through a minimum. The idea seemed rather revolutionary to persons reared—as we had been—in houses with halls in them. Still, this person spoke as one having authority and we would listen with due respect to his words as he went on:

"All right, then, we'll consider the hallway as chopped out. By chopping it out that gives us a chance to put the dining room here in this place and give a vista through into the living room. Here, I'll show you exactly what I mean—what did I do with my lead pencil? Because no matter what else you do or do not have, you must have a vista through."

Before he had finished with this alteration and taken up with the next one we were made to understand that a house without a vista through was substantially the same as no house at all. Ashamed that we had been guilty of so gross an oversight, I would make a note, "Vista through," on a scratch pad which I kept for that very purpose. Under the spell of his eloquence and compelling personality, I had already decided that first we would build a vista through, and then after that if any money was left we would sort of flank the vista through with bedrooms and a kitchen and other things of a comparatively incidental nature.

Having scored this important point, the king of the pouncers—now warming to his work and with his eyes feverishly lit by the enthusiasm of the zealot—would proceed to claw the quivering giblets out of another section of our plan. Hark to him:

"And say, see here now, how about your sun parlor? I can see two—no, three places suitable for tacking on a sun parlor merely by moving some walls round and putting the main entrance at the east front instead of the south front—funny the architect didn't think of that! He should have thought of that the very first thing if he calls himself a regular architect—and I suppose he does. What's the idea, leaving off the sun parlor?"

Then weakly, with an inner sinking of the heart, we would confess that we had not calculated on including any sun parlors in the general scope and he for his part would proceed to show us how deadly an omission, how grievous an offense this would be.

It is a curious psychological paradox that we dreaded these suggestions and yet welcomed them, too. That is to say, we would begin by dreading them—resenting them would perhaps be a better term—and invariably would wind up by welcoming them. Nevertheless, there were times when I gave my celebrated imitation of the turning worm. Jarred off my mental balance by a proposed change which seemed entirely contrary to the trend of the style of house we had in mind for our house, I would offer at the outset a faint counter argument in defense, especially if a notion which was about to be offered as a sacrifice on the altar of friendly counsel had been a favorite little idea of my own—one that I had found in my own head, as the saying went in the Army. Though knowing in advance that I was fighting a losing fight, I would raise a meek small voice in protest. Never once did my protesting avail. There was one stock answer which my fellow controversialist always had handy—ready to belt me with.

"One moment!" he would say, smiling the superior half-pitying smile which was really responsible for Cain's killing Abel that time.

Abel smiled just exactly in that way and so Cain killed him, and if you're asking me, he got exactly what was coming to him. "One moment!" he would say. "You've never built a house before, have you?"

"No," I would confess, "but—but—"

"Then, pardon me, but I have! What I am trying to do is to keep you from making the mistakes I made. Almost anybody will make mistakes building his first house. I only wish I'd had somebody round to advise me as I'm advising you before I O. K.'d the plans and signed the contract. As it was, it cost me four thousand dollars to pull out two walls so that we could have a sun parlor. If you go ahead and build your house without having a sun parlor you'll never regret it but once—and that'll be all the time you live in it. Look here now, while I show you how easily you can do it." And so on and so forth until we would capitulate and I'd write "Memo—sun parlor, sure," on my little pad.

Take for example the matter of sleeping porches. Personally I have never been drawn greatly to the idea of sleeping outdoors. I used to think an outdoor bedroom must be almost as inconvenient as an outdoor bathroom, and with me bathing has always been a solitary pleasure. I have felt that I would not be at my best while bathing before an audience. That may denote selfishness on my part, but such is my nature and I cannot change it. I suppose this prejudice against bathing before a crowd is constitutional with me—hereditary, as it were. All my folks were awfully peculiar that way.

When they felt that they needed bathing they also felt that they needed privacy. I sometimes think that my family must have been descended from Susanna. She was a Biblical lady and so did not have any last name, but you probably recall her from the circumstance of her having been surprised while bathing by two snoopy elders. Whenever one of the Old Masters ran out of other subjects to paint, he would paint a picture of Susanna and the elders. In no two of their pictures did she look alike, but in all of them that I've ever seen she looked embarrassed. Yes, I dare say Susanna was our direct ancestress. Like practically all Southern families, ours is a very old family and I've always been led to believe that we go back a long way. True, I've never heard the Old Testament mentioned in this connection, but in view of the fact of our family being such an old or Southern family I reckon it is but fair to presume that we go back fully that far if not farther.

Indeed I have been told that in my infancy a friend of the family, a man who had delved rather into archeology, on calling one day remarked that I had a head shaped exactly like a cuneiform Chaldean brick. It was years later, however, before my parents learned what a cuneiform Chaldean brick looked like and by that time the person who had paid me the compliment was dead and it was too late to take offense at him. And anyhow, in the meantime the contour of my skull had so altered that it was now possible for me to wear a regular child's hat bought out of a store. I point out the circumstance merely as possible collateral evidence showing semiprehistoric hereditary influences to corroborate the more or less direct evidence that as a family we antedate nearly all—if not all—of these Northern families by going back into the very dawn of civilization. I have a great aunt who rather specializes in genealogies and especially our own genealogy and the next time I see her I mean to ask her to consult the authorities and find out whether there is a strain of the Susanna blood in our stock. If she confirms my present belief that there is I shall be very glad to let everybody know about it in an appendix to the next edition of this work.

As with taking a bath outdoors, so with sleeping outdoors; this always was my profound conviction. I had a number of arguments, all good arguments I thought, to offer in support of my position. To begin with, I am what might be called a sincere sleeper, a whole-souled sleeper. I have been told that when I am sleeping and the windows are open everybody in the vicinity knows I am actually sleeping and not lying there tossing about restlessly upon my bed. I would not go so far as to say that I snore, but like most deep thinkers I breathe heavily when asleep. On board a sleeping car I have been known to breathe even more heavily than the locomotive did. I know of this only by hearsay, but when twenty or thirty passengers, all strangers to you, unite in a common statement to the same effect you are bound to admit, if you have any sense of fairness in your make-up, that there must be an element of truth in what they allege.

Very well, then, let us concede that I sleep with the muffler cut out open. In view of this fact I have felt that I would not care to sleep in the open where my style of sleeping might invite adverse comment. In such a matter I try to have a proper consideration for the feelings of others.

Indeed I carried it to such a point that when we lived in the closely congested city, with neighboring flat dwellers just across a narrow courtyard, I placed the head of my bed in such a position that I might do the bulk of my breathing up the chimney.

Besides—so I was wont to argue—what in thunder was the good of having a comfortable cozy bedroom with steam heat and everything in it, and a night lamp for reading if one felt like reading, and a short cut down to the pantry if one felt hungry in the small hours, and then on a cold night deliberately to crawl out on a wind-swept porch hung against the outer wall of the house and sleep there? I once knew one of these sleeping-porch fiends who was given to boasting that in wintertime he often woke to find the snow had drifted in on the top of him while he slept. He professed to like the sensation; he bragged about it. From his remarks you gleaned that his idea of a really attractive boudoir was the polar bear's section up at the Bronx Zoo. I was sorry his name had not been Moe instead of Joe—which was what it was—because if it had only been the former I had thought up a clever play on words. I was going to catch him in company and trap him into boasting about loving to sleep in a snowdrift and then I was going to call him Eskimo, which should have been good for a laugh every time it was spontaneously sprung on a fresh audience.

In short, taking one thing with another, I have never favored sleeping porches. But after listening to friends who either had them or who were so sorry they didn't have them that they were determined we should have a full set of them on our house, we concurred in the consensus of opinion and decided to cast aside old prejudices and to have them at all hazards. I believe in the rule of the majority—of course with a few private reservations from time to time, as for instance, when the majority gets carried away by this bone-dry notion.

I recall in particular one friend who was especially emphatic and especially convincing in the details of offering suggestions and advice, and—where he deemed such painful measures necessary—in administering reproof for and correction of our faulty misconceptions of what a house should be. But then he was a Bostonian by birth and a Harvard graduate and had the manner—shall we call it the slightly superior manner?—which so often marks one who may boast these two qualifications. When you meet a well-bred native Bostonian who has been through Harvard it is as though you had met an egg which had enjoyed the unique distinction of having been laid twice and both times successfully. Our friend was distinctly that way. When he had rendered judgment there was no human appeal. It never occurred to us there could be any appeal.

So we incorporated sleeping porches and vistas through and sun parlors and a hundred other things—more or less—into the plan. Obeying the wills of stronger natures than ours, we figuratively knocked out walls and then on subsequent and what appeared to be superior counsel figuratively stuck them back in again. We lifted the roof for air and we lowered it for style. We tiled the floors and then untiled them and put down beautiful mental hardwood all over the place. We rejected paneled wainscotings in favor of rough-cast plaster and then abolished the plaster for something in the nature of a smooth finish for our walls. By direction we tacked on an ell here and an annex there. If we had kept all the additions which at one period or another we were quite sure we must keep in order to make our home complete we should have had a house entirely unsuitable for persons of our position in life to reside in, but could have made considerable sums of money by renting it out for national conventions.

On one point and only one point did we remain adamant. Otherwise we were as clay in the hands of the potter, as flax to the loom of the weaver; but there we were as adamant as an ant. We concurred in the firm and unswervable decision that—no matter what else we might have or might not have in our house—we would not have a den in it. By den I mean one of those cubby-holes opening off a living room or an entrance hall that is fitted up with woolly hangings and an Oriental smoking set where people are supposed to go and sit when they wish to be comfortable—only nobody in his right mind ever does. In my day I have done too much traveling on the Pullman of commerce to crave to have a section of one in my home. Call them dens if you will; I know a sleeping-car compartment when I see it, even though it be thinly disguised by a pair of trading-stamp scimitars crossed over the door and a running yard of mailorder steins up on a shelf. Several earnest advocates of the den theory tried their persuasive powers on us, but each time one or the other of us turned a deaf ear. When her deaf ear was tired from turning I would turn mine a while, and vice versa. There is no den in our home. Except over my dead body there never shall be one.

While on this general subject I may add that if anybody succeeds in sticking a Japanese catalpa on our lawn it will also be necessary to remove my lifeless but still mutely protesting remains before going ahead with the planting. I have accepted the new state income tax in the spirit in which it seems to be meant—namely, to confiscate any odd farthings that may still be knocking round the place after the Federal income tax has been paid, and a very sound notion, too. What is money for if it isn't for legislators to spend? Should the Prohibitionists put through the seizure-and-search law as a national measure I suppose in time I may get accustomed to waking up and finding a zealous gent with a badge and one of those long prehensile noses especially adapted for poking into other people's businesses, such as so many professional uplifters have, prowling through the place on the lookout for a small private bottle labeled "Spirits Aromatic Ammonia,

Aged in the Wood." With the passage of time I may become really enthusiastic over the prospect of having my baggage ransacked for contraband essences every time I cross the state line. My taste in pyjamas has been favorably commented on and there is no reason why my fellow travelers should not enjoy a treat as the inspector dumps the contents of the top tray out on the car floor. The main thing is to get used to whatever it is that we have got to get used to.

But I have a profound conviction that in the matter of a Japanese catalpa on the lawn, just as in the matter of a den opening off the living room and taking up the space which otherwise would make a first-rate umbrella-and-galosh closet, I could never hope to get used. Nor do I yearn for a weeping mulberry tree about the premises. I dislike its prevalent shape and the sobbing sound it makes when especially moved by the distress which chronically afflicts the sensitive thing. Nature endowed our abandoned farm with a plenteous selection of certain deciduous growths common to the temperate zone—elms and maples and black walnuts and hickories and beeches and birches and dogwoods and locusts; also pines and hemlocks and cedars and spruces. What the good Lord designed as suitable arboreal adornment for the eastern seaboard is good enough for me. I have no desire to clutter up the small section of North America to which I hold the title deeds with trees which do not match in with the rest of North America. I should as soon think of putting a pagoda on top of Pike's Peak or connecting the Thousand Islands with a system of pergolas.

Having got that out of my system, let us get off the grounds and back to the house proper. As I was remarking just before being diverted from the main line, a den was about the only voluntary offering which we positively refused to take over. Every other notion of whatsoever nature was duly adopted and duly carried on to the architect He was a wonderful man. All architects, I am convinced, must be wonderful men, but him I would call one of the pick of his breed. How he managed to make practical use of some of the ideas we brought to him and fit them into the plan; how without hurting our feelings or the feelings of our friends he succeeded in curing us of sundry delusions we had acquired; how he succeeded in confining the ground plan to a scale which would not make the New York Public Library seem in comparison a puny and inconsequential edifice; and how taking a number of the suggestions which came to him and rejecting the others he yet preserved the structural balance and the suitable proportions which he had had in his mind all along—these, to my way of thinking, approximate the Eighth Wonder. No, it is the first wonder; the remaining seven finish place, show and also ran.

After a season of debate, compromise and conciliation, when the gray in his hair had perceptibly thickened and the lines in his face had deepened, though still he wore his chronic patient smile which makes strangers like him, the final specifications were blue-printed and the work was started. A lady to whom I have the honor of being very closely related by marriage removed the first shovel load of loam from the contemplated excavation. She is not what you would call a fancy shoveler and the net result of her labor, I should say offhand, was about a heaping dessert-spoonful of topsoil. Had I guessed what that inconsequential pinch of earth would subsequently mean to us in joy I should have put it in a snuffbox and carried it about with me as the first tangible souvenir of a great accomplishment and a reminder to me never again to look slightingly upon small things. Bulk does not necessarily imply ultimate achievement. If Tom Thumb had been two feet taller and eighteen inches broader than he was I doubt whether he would amounted to much as a dwarf.

Well, we reared the foundations and then one fine April morning our country abandoned its policy of watchful waiting for one of swatful hating. While we were at war it did not seem patriotic to try to go ahead. There was another reason—a variety of reasons rather. Very soon labor was not to be had, or materials either. Take the detail of concrete. Now that the last war is over and the next war not as yet started, I violate no confidence and betray no trust in stating that one of our chief military secrets had to do with this seemingly harmless product. We were shooting concrete at the Germans. In large quantities it was fatal; in small, mussy. And while the Germans were digging the gummy stuff out of their eyes and their hair our fellows would swarm over the top and capture them. And if you are not sure that I am telling the exact truth regarding this I only wish you had tried during active hostilities—as I did—to buy a few jorums and noggins of concrete. Trying would have made a true believer of you, too. And the same might be said for steel girders and cow hair to put into plaster so it will stick, and ten-penny nails. We were firing all these things at the enemy. It must have disconcerted him terribly to be expecting high explosives and have a keg of ten-penny nails or a bale of cow hair burst in his midst. Without desire to detract from the glory of the other branches of the service, I am of the opinion that it was ten-penny nails that won the war. And in bringing about this splendid result I did my share by not buying any in large amount for going on eighteen months.

I couldn't.

War having come and concrete having gone, the contractor on our little job knocked off operations until such time as Germany had been cured of what principally ailed her. Even through the delay, though, we found pleasure in our project. We would perch perilously upon the top of the jagged walls and enjoy the view the while we imagined we sat in our finished dream house. We could see it, even if no one else could. In rainy weather we brought umbrellas along. The fact that a passerby beheld us thus on a showery afternoon I suppose was responsible for the report which spread through the vicinity that a couple of lunatics were roosting on some stone ruins halfway up the side of Mott's Mountain. We didn't mind though. The great creators of this world have ever been the victims of popular misunderstanding. Sir Isaak Walton, sitting under an apple tree and through the falling of an apple discovering the circulation of the blood, is to us a splendid figure of genius; but I have no doubt the neighbors said at the time that he would have been much better employed helping Mrs. W. with the housework. And probably there was a lot of loose and scornful talk when Benjamin Franklin went out in a thunderstorm with a kite and a brass key and fussed round among the darting lightning bolts until he was as wet as a rag and then came home and tried to dry his sopping feet before one of those old-fashioned open fireplaces so common in that period. But what was the result? The Franklin heater—that's what. With such historic examples behind us, what cared we though the tongue of slander wagged while we inhabited our site with the leaky heavens for a roof to our parlor and the far horizons for its wall. Not to every one is vouchsafed the double boon of spending long happy days in one's home and at the same time keeping out in the open air.

On the day the United Press scooped the opposition by announcing the cessation of hostilities some days before the hostilities really cessated, thereby scoring one of the greatest journalistic beats since the Millerites prognosticated the end of the world, giving day, date and hour somewhat prematurely in advance of that interesting event, which as a matter of fact has not taken place yet—on that memorable day the country at large celebrated the advent of peace. We also celebrated the peace, but on a personal account we celebrated something else besides. We celebrated the prospect of an early resumption of work in the construction of our house.

During the months that followed I learned a lot about the intricacies and the mysteries of house building. Beforehand, in my ignorance I figured that the preliminary plans might be stretched out or contracted in to suit the shifting mood of the designer and the sudden whim of his client, but that once the walls went up and the beams went across and the rafters came down both parties were thereafter bound by set metes and bounds. Not at all. I discovered that there is nothing more plastic than brickwork, nothing more elastic than a girder. A carpenter spends days of his time and dollars of your money fitting and joining a certain section of framework; that is to say, he engages in such craftsmanship when not sharpening his saw. It has been my observation that the average conscientious carpenter allows forty per cent of his eight-hour day to saw sharpening. It must be a joy to him to be able to give so much time daily to putting nice keen teeth in a saw, knowing that somebody else is paying him for it at the rate of ninety cents an hour. Watching him at work in intervals between saw filing, you get from him the impression that unless this particular angle of the wooden skeleton is articulated just so the whole structure will come tumbling down some day when least expected. At length he gets the job done to his satisfaction and goes elsewhere.

Along comes a steamfitter and he, whistling merrily the while, takes a chisel or an adze or an ax and just bodaciously haggles a large ragged orifice in the carpenter's masterpiece. Through the hole he runs a Queen Rosamond's maze of iron pipes. He then departs and the carpenter is called back to the scene of the mutilation. After sharpening his saw some more in a restrained and contemplative manner, he patches up the wound as best he can. Enter, then, the boss plumber accompanied by a helper. The boss plumber finds a comfortable two-by-four to sit on and does sit thereon and lights up his pipe and while he smokes and directs operations the assistant or understudy, with edged tools provided for that purpose, tears away some of the cadaver's most important ribs and several joints of its spinal column for the forthcoming insertion of various concealed fixtures.

Following the departure of these assassins the patient carpenter returns and to the best of his ability reduces all the compound fractures that he conveniently can get at, following which he sharpens his saw—not the big saw which he sharpened from eight-forty-five to ten-fifteen o'clock this morning, but the little buttonhole saw which he has not sharpened since yesterday afternoon; this done, he calls it a day and goes home to teach his little son Elmer, who expects to follow in the paternal footsteps, the rudiments of the art of filing a saw without being in too much of a hurry about it, which after all is the main point in this department of the carpentering profession.

And the next day the plumber remembers where he left his sack of smoking tobacco, or the steam fitter's attention is directed to the fact that when he stuck in the big pipe like a bass tuba he forgot to insert alongside it the little pipe like a piccolo, and therefore it becomes necessary to maltreat the already thrice-mangled remains of woodwork. A month or so later the plasterers arrive—they were due in a week, but a plasterer who showed up when he was expected or any time within a month after he had solemnly promised on his sacred word of honor that he meant to show up would have his card taken away from him and be put out of the union. Hours after Gabriel has blown his trump for the last call it is going to be incumbent upon the little angel bell hops to go and page the plasterers, else they won't get there for judgment at all.

Be that as it may and undoubtedly will be, in a month or so the plasterers arrive, wearing in streaks the same effects in laid-on complexion that so many of our leading débutantes are wearing all over their faces. The chief plasterer looks over the prospect and decides that in order to insure a smooth and unbroken surface for his plaster coat the plumbing and the heating connections must have their elbows tucked in a few notches, which ultimatum naturally requires the good offices of the carpenter, first to snatch out and afterward to hammer back into some sort of alignment the shreds and fragments of his original job. When this sort of thing, with variations, has gone on through a period of months, a house has become an intricate and complicated fabric of patchworks and mosaics held together, as nearly as a layman can figure, by the power of cohesion and the pressures of dead weights. The amazing part of it is that it stays put. I am quite sure that our house will stay put, because despite the vagaries—perhaps I should say the morbid curiosity—of various artificers intent on taking the poor thing apart every little while, it was constructed of materials which as humans compute mutabilities are reasonably permanent in their basic characters.

It was our desire to have a new house that would look like an old house; a yearning in which the architect heartily concurred, he having a distaste for the slick, shiny, look-out-for-the-paint look which is common enough in American country houses. In this ambition a combination of circumstances served our ends. For the lower walls we looted two of the ancient stone fences which meandered aimlessly across the face of our acres. According to local tradition, those fences dated back to pre-Revolutionary days; they were bearded thick with lichens and their faces were scored and seamed. In laying them up we were fortunate enough to find and hire a stonemason who was part artificer but mostly real artist—an Italian, with the good taste in masonry which seems to be inherent in his countrymen; only in this case the good taste was developed to a very high degree. Literally he would fondle a stone whose color and contour appealed to him and his final dab with the trowel of mortar was in the nature of a caress.

On top of this find came another and even luckier one. Three miles away was an abandoned brickyard. Once an extensive busy plant, it had lain idle for many years. Lately it had been sold and the new owners were now preparing to salvage the material it contained. Thanks to the forethought of the architect, we secured the pick of these pickings. From old pits we exhumed fine hard brick which had been stacked there for a generation, taking on those colors and that texture which only long exposure to wind and rain and sun can give to brick. These went into our upper walls. For a lower price than knotty, wavy, fresh-cut, half-green spruce would have cost us at a lumber yard, modern prices and lumber yards being what they are, we stripped from the old kiln sheds beautiful clear North Carolina boards, seasoned and staunch. These were for the rough flooring and the sheathing. The same treasure mine provided us with iron bars for reënforcing; with heavy beams and splendid thick wide rafters; with fire brick glazed over by clays and minerals which in a molten state had flowed down their surfaces; with girders and underpinnings of better grade and greater weight than any housebuilder of moderate means can afford these times. Finally, for roofing we procured old field slates of all colors and thicknesses and all sizes; and these by intent were laid on in irregular catch-as-catch-can fashion, suggestive when viewed at a little distance of the effect of thatching. Another Italian, a wood carver this time, craftily cut the scrolled beam ends which show beneath our friendly eaves and in the shadows of our gables. It was necessary only to darken with stains the newly gouged surfaces; the rest had been antiquated already by fifty years of Hudson River climate. Before the second beam was in place a wren was building her nest on the sloped top of the first one. We used to envy that wren—she had moved in before we had.

VII

"And Sold To—"

When the house was up as far as the second floor and the first mortgage, talk rose touching on the furnishings. To me it seemed there would be ample time a decade or so thence to begin thinking of the furnishings. So far as I could tell there was no hurry and probably there never would be any hurry. For the job had reached that stage so dismally familiar to any one who ever started a house with intent to live in it when completed, if ever. I refer to the stage when a large and variegated assortment of hired help are ostensibly busy upon the premises and yet everything seems practically to be at a standstill. From the standpoint of a mere bystander whose only function is to pay the bills, it seems that the workmen are only coming to the job of a morning because they hate the idea of hanging round their own homes all day with nothing to do.

So it was with us. Sawing and hammering and steam fitting and plumbing and stone-lying and brick-lying were presumed to be going on; laborers were wielding the languid pick; a roof layer was defying the laws of gravitation on our ridgepole; at stated intervals there were great gobs of payments on account of this or that to be met and still and yet and notwithstanding, to the lay eye the progress appeared infinitesimal. For the first time I could understand why Pharaoh or Rameses or whoever it was that built the Pyramids displayed peevishness toward the Children of Israel. Indeed I developed a cordial sympathy for him. He had my best wishes. They were four or five thousand years late, but even so he had 'em and welcome.

Accordingly when the matter of investing in furnishings was broached I stoutly demurred. As I recall, I spoke substantially as follows:

"Why all this mad haste? Rome wasn't built in a day, as I have often heard, and in view of my own recent experiences I am ready to make affidavit to the fact. I'll go further than that. I'll bet any sum within reason, up to a million dollars, that the meanest smokehouse in Rome was not built in a day. No Roman smokehouse—Ionic, Doric, Corinthian or Old Line Etruscan—is barred. Unless workingmen have changed a whole lot since those times, it was not possible to begin to start to commence to get ready to go ahead to proceed to advance with that smokehouse or any other smokehouse in a day. And after they did get started they dallied along and dallied along and killed time until process curing came into fashion among the best families of Ancient Rome and smokehouses lost their vogue altogether. Let us not be too impetuous about the detail of furnishings. I have a feeling—a feeling based on my own observations over yonder at the site of our own little undertaking—that when that house is really done the only furnishings we'll require will be a couple of wheel chairs and something to warm up spoon victuals in.

"Anyhow, what's wrong with the furnishings we already have in storage? Judging by the present rate of non-progress—of static advancement, if I may use such a phrase—long before we have a place to set them up in our furnishings will be so entirely out of style that they'll be back in style all over again, if you get me. These things move in cycles, you know. One generation buys furniture and uses it. The next generation finding it hopelessly old-fashioned and out of date burns it up or casts it away or gives it away or stores it in the attic—anything to get rid of it. The third generation spends vast sums of money trying to restore it or the likes of it, for by that time the stuff which was despised and discarded is in strong demand and fetching fancy prices.

"The only mistake is to belong to the middle generation, which curiously enough is always the present one. We crave what our grandparents owned but our parents did not. Our grandchildren will crave what we had but our own children won't. They'll junk it. To-day's monstrosity is day-after-tomorrow's art treasure just as today's museum piece is day-before-yesterday's monstrosity. Therefore, I repeat, let us remain calm. I figure that when we actually get into that house our grandchildren will be of a proper age to appreciate the belongings now appertaining to us, and all will be well."

Thus in substance I spoke. The counter argument offered was that—conceding what I said to be true—the fact remained and was not to be gainsaid that we did not have anywhere near enough of furnishings to equip the house we hoped at some distant date to occupy.

"You must remember," I was told, "that for the six or eight years before we decided to move out here to the country we lived in a flat."

"What of it?" I retorted instantly. "What of it?" I repeated, for when in the heat of controversy I think up an apt bit of repartee like that I am apt to utter it a second time for the sake of emphasis. Pausing only to see if my stroke of instantaneous retort had struck in, I continued:

"That last flat we had swallowed up furniture as a rat hole swallows sand. First and last we must have poured enough stuff into that flat to furnish the state of Rhode Island. And what about the monthly statements we are getting now from the storage warehouse signed by the president of the company, old man Pl. Remit? Doesn't the size of them prove that in the furniture-owning line at least we are to be regarded as persons of considerable consequence?"

"Don't be absurd," I was admonished. "Just compare the size of the largest bedroom in that last flat we had in One Hundred and Tenth Street with the size of the smallest bedroom we expect to have in the new place. Why, you could put the biggest bedroom we had there into the smallest bedroom we are going to have here and lose it! And then think of the halls we must furnish and the living room and the breakfast porch and everything. Did we have a breakfast porch in the flat? We did not! Did we have a living room forty feet one way and twenty-eight the other? We did not! Did we have a dining room in that flat that was big enough to swing a cat in?"

"We didn't have any cat."

"All the same, we—"

"I doubt whether any of the neighbors would have loaned us a cat just for that purpose." I felt I had the upper hand and I meant to keep it. "Besides, you know I don't like cats. What is the use of importing foreign matters such as cats—and purely problematical cats at that—into a discussion about something else? What relation does a cat bear to furniture, I ask you? Still, speaking of cats, I'm reminded—"

"Never mind trying to be funny. And never mind trying to steer the conversation off the right track either. Please pay attention to what I am saying—let's see, where was I? Oh, yes: Did we have a hall in that flat worthy to be dignified by the name of a hall? We did not! We had a passageway—that's what it was—a passageway. Now there is a difference between furnishing a mere passageway and a regular hall, as you are about to discover before you are many months older."

On second thought I had to concede there was something in what had just been said. One could not have swung one's cat in our dining room in the flat with any expectation of doing the cat any real good. And the hallway we had in our flat was like nearly all halls in New York flats. It was comfortably filled when you hung a watercolor picture up on its wall and uncomfortably crowded if you put a clarionet in the corner. It would have been bad luck to open an umbrella anywhere in our flat—bad luck for the umbrella if for nothing else. Despite its enormous capacity for inhaling furniture it had been, when you came right down to cases, a form-fitting flat. So mentally confessing myself worsted at this angle of the controversy, I fell back on my original argument that certainly it would be years and years and it might be forever before we possibly could expect—at the current rate of speed of the building operations, or speaking exactly, at the current rate of the lack of speed—to move in.

"But the architect has promised us on his solemn word of honor—"

"Don't tell me what the architect has promised!" I said bitterly. "Next to waiters, architects are the most optimistic creatures on earth. A waiter is always morally certain that twenty minutes is the extreme limit of time that will be required to cook anything. You think that you would like, say, to have a fish that is not listed on the bill of fare under the subheading 'Ready Dishes'—it may be a whale or it may be a minnow: that detail makes no difference to him—and you ask the waiter how about it, and he is absolutely certain that it will be possible to borrow a fishing pole somewhere and dig bait and send out and catch that fish and bring it back in and clean it and take the scales and the fins off and garnish it with sprigs of parsley and potatoes and lemon and make some drawn butter sauce to pour over it and bring it to you in twenty minutes. If he didn't think so he would not be a waiter. An architect is exactly like a waiter, except that he thinks in terms of days instead of terms of minutes. Don't tell me about architects! I only wish I were as sure of heaven as the average architect is regarding that which no mortal possibly can be sure of, labor conditions being what chronically they are."

But conceded that the reader is but a humble husbandman—meaning by that a man who is married—he doubtless has already figured out the result of this debate. Himself, he knows how such debates usually do terminate. In the end I surrendered, and the final upshot was that we set about the task of furnishing the rooms that were to be. From that hour dated the beginning of my wider and fuller education into the system commonly in vogue these times in or near the larger cities along our Atlantic seaboard for the furnishing of homes. I have learned though. It has cost me a good deal of time and some money and my nervous system is not what it was, having suffered a series of abrupt shocks, but I have learned. I know something now—not much, but a little—about period furniture.

A period, as you may recall, is equal to a full stop; in fact a period is a full stop. This is a rule in punctuation which applies in other departments of life, as I have discovered. Go in extensively for the period stuff in your interior equipments and presently you will be coming to a full stop in your funds on hand. The thing works out the same way every time. I care not how voluminously large and plethoric your cash balance may be, period furniture carried to an excess will convert it into a recent site and then the bank will be sending you one of those little printed notices politely intimating that "your account appears overdrawn." And any time a banker goes so far as to hint that your account appears overdrawn you may bet the last cent you haven't left that he is correct. He knows darned good and well it is overdrawn and this merely is his kindly way of softening the blow to you.

I have a theory that when checks begin to roll in from the clearing house made out to this or that dealer in period furniture the paying teller hastens to the adjusting department to see how your deposits seem to be bearing up under the strain. It is as though he heard you were buying oil stocks or playing the races out of your savings and he might as well begin figuring now about how long approximately it will be before your account will become absolutely vacant in appearance.

As I was remarking, I know a trifle about period furniture. Offhand now, I can distinguish a piece which dates back to Battle Abbey from something which goes back no farther than Battle Creek. Before I could not do this. I was forever getting stuff of the time of the Grand Monarch confused with something right fresh out of Grand Rapids. Generally speaking, all antiques—whether handed down from antiquity or made on the premises—looked alike to me. But in the light of my painfully acquired knowledge I now can see the difference almost at a glance. Sometimes I may waver a trifle. I look at a piece of furniture which purports to be an authentic antique. It is decrepit and creaky and infirm; the upholstering is frayed and faded and stained; the legs are splayed and tottery; the seams gape and there are cracks in the paneling. If it is a chair, no plump person in his or her right mind would dare sit down in it. If it is a bedstead, any sizable adult undertaking to sleep in it would do so at his peril. So, outwardly and visibly it seems to bear the stamp of authenticity. Yet still I doubt. It may be a craftily devised counterfeit. It may be something of comparatively recent manufacture which has undergone careless handling. In such a case I seek for the wormholes—if any—the same as any other seasoned collector would.

Up until comparatively recently wormholes, considered as such, had no great lure to me. If I thought of them at all I thought of them as a topic which was rather lacking in interest to begin with and one easily exhausted. If you had asked me about wormholes I—speaking offhand—probably would say that this was a matter which naturally might appeal to a worm but would probably hold forth no great attraction for a human being, unless he happened to be thinking of going fishing. But this was in my more ignorant, cruder days, before I took a beginner's easy course in the general science of wormholes. I am proud of my progress, but I would not go so far just yet as to say that I am a professional. Still I am out of the amateur class. I suppose you might call me a semi-pro, able under ordinary circumstances to do any given wormhole in par.

For example, at present I have an average of three correct guesses out of five chances—which is a very high average for one who but a little while ago was the veriest novice at distinguishing between ancient wormholes, as made by a worm, and modern wormholing done by piece-work. I cannot explain to you just how I do this—it is a thing which after a while just seems to come to you. But of course you must have a natural gift for it to start with—an inherent affinity for wormholes, as it were.

However, I will say that I did not thoroughly master the cardinal principles of this art until after I had studied under one of the leading wormhole experts in this country—a man who has devoted years of his life just to wormholes. True, like most great specialists he is a person of one idea. Get him off of wormholes and the conversation is apt to drag, but discussing his own topic he can go on for hours and hours. I really believe he gets more pleasure out of one first-class, sixteenth-century wormhole than the original worm did. And as Kipling would say: I learned about wormholes from him.

At the outset I must confess I rather leaned toward a nice, neat, up-to-date wormhole as produced amid sanitary surroundings in an inspected factory out in Michigan, where no scab wormholes would be tolerated, rather than toward one which had been done by an unorganized foreign worm—possibly even a pauperized worm—two or three hundred years ago, when there was no such thing as a closed shop and no protection against germs. Whenever possible I believe in patronizing the products of union labor. But the expert speedily set me right on this point. He made me see that in furnishings and decorations nothing modern can possibly compare with something which is crumbly and tottery with the accumulated weight of the hoary years.

He taught me about patina, too. Patina is a most fascinating subject, once you get thoroughly into it. Everybody who goes in for period furniture must get into it sooner or later, and the sooner the better, because if you are not able to recognize patina at a glance you are as good as lost when you undertake to appraise antique furniture. When a connoisseur lays hold upon a piece of furniture alleged to have rightful claims to antiquity the first thing he does is to run his hand along the exposed surfaces to ascertain by the practiced touch of his fingers whether the patina is on the level or was applied by a crafty counterfeiter. After that he upends it to look for the wormholes. If both are orthodox he gives it his validation as the genuine article. If they are not he brands the article a spurious imitation and rejects it with ill-concealed scorn. There are other tests, but these two are the surest ones.

For the benefit of those who may not have had any advantages as recently and expensively enjoyed I will state that patina is the gloss or film which certain sorts of metal and certain sorts of polished woods acquire through age, long usage and wear. With the passage of time fabrics also may acquire it. You may have noticed it in connection with a pair of black diagonal trousers that had seen long and severe wear or on the elbows of summer-before-last's blue serge coat. However, patina in pants or on the braided seams of a presiding elder's Sunday suit is not so highly valued as when it occurs in relation to a Jacobean church pew or a William-and-Mary what-not.

When I look back on my untutored state before we began to patronize the antique shops and the auction shops I am ashamed—honestly I am. The only excuse I can offer is based on the grounds of my earlier training. Like so many of my fellow countrymen, born and reared as I was in the crude raw atmosphere of interior America—anyhow, almost any wealthy New Yorker will tell you it is a crude raw atmosphere and not in any way to be compared with the refined atmosphere which is about the only thing you can get for nothing in Europe—as I say, brought up as I was amid such raw surroundings and from the cradle made the unconscious victim of this environment, I had an idea that when a person craved furniture he went for it to a regular furniture store having ice boxes and porch hammocks and unparalleled bargains in golden oak dining-room sets in the show windows, and there he made his selection and gave his order and paid a deposit down and the people at the shop sent it up to his house in a truck with historic scenes such as Washington Crossing the Delaware and Daniel in the Lions' Den painted on the sides of the truck, and after that he had nothing to worry about in connection with the transaction except the monthly installments.

You see, I date back to the Rutherford B. Hayes period of American architecture and applied designing—a period which had a solid background of mid-Victorian influence with a trace of Philadelphia Centennial running through it, being bounded at the farther end by such sterling examples of parlor statuary as the popular pieces respectively entitled, "Welcoming the New Minister," "Bringing Home the Bride," and "Baby's First Bath," and bounded at the nearer end by burnt-wood plaques and frames for family portraits with plush insets and hand-painted flowers on the moldings. By the conceptions of those primitive times nothing so set off the likeness of a departed great-aunt as a few red-plush insets.

Some of my most cherished boyhood memories centered about bird's-eye-maple bedroom sets and parlor furniture of heavy black walnut trimmed in a manner which subsequently came to be popular among undertakers for the adornment of the casket when they had orders to spare no expense for a really fashionable or—as the saying went then—a tony funeral. Tony subsequently became nobby and nobby is now swagger, but though the idioms change with the years the meaning remains the same. When the parlor was opened for a formal occasion—it remained closed while the ordinary life of the household went on—its interior gave off a rich deep turpentiny smell like a paint-and-varnish store on a hot day. And the bird's-eye maple, as I recall, had a high slick finish which, however, did not dim the staring, unwinking effect of the round knots which so plentifully dappled its graining. Lying on the bed and contemplating the footboard gave one the feeling that countless eyes were looking at one, which in those days was regarded as highly desirable.

I remember all our best people favored bird's-eye maple for the company room. They clung to it, too. East Aurora had a hard struggle before it made any noticeable impress upon the decorative tendencies of West Kentucky, for we were a conservative breed and slow to take up the mission styles featuring armchairs weighing a couple of hundred pounds apiece and art-craft designs in hammered metals and semi-tanned leathers. Moreover, a second-hand shop in our town was not an antique shop; it was what its name implied—a second-hand shop. You didn't go there to buy things you wanted, but to sell things you did not want.

So in view of these youthful influences it should be patent to all that, having other things to think of—such, for example, as making a living—I did not realize that in New York at least those wishful of following the modes did not go to a good live shop making a specialty of easy payments when they had a house-furnishing proposition on their hands. That might be all very well for the pedestrian classes and for those living in the remote districts who kept a mail-order catalogue on the center table and wrote on from time to time with the money order enclosed.

I soon was made to understand that the really correct thing was first of all to call in a professional decorator, if one could afford it. A professional decorator is a person of either sex who can think up more ways and quicker ways of spending other people's money than the director of a shipping board can. But whether you retained the services of a regular decorator or elected to struggle along on your own, you went for your purchases to specialty shops or to antique shops, or—best of all—to the smart auction shops on or hard by Fifth Avenue and Madison Avenue.

Than the auction rooms in the Fifth Avenue district I know of no places better adapted for studying patina, wormholing and human nature in a variety of interesting phases. To such an establishment, on the days when a sale is announced—which means two or three times a week for a good part of the year—repair wealthy patrons, patrons who were wealthy before the mania for bidding in things came upon them, as it does come upon so many, and patrons who are trying to look as though they were wealthy. The third group are in the majority.

Amateur collectors come, on the lookout for lace fans or Japanese bronzes or Chinese ceramics or furniture or pictures or hangings or rugs or tapestries, or whatever it is that constitutes their favorite hobby. There are sure to be prominent actor folk and author folk in this category. Dealers are on hand, each as wise looking as a barnful of hoot-owls and talking the jargon of the craft.

Agents from rival auction houses are sometimes seen, ready, should the opportunity present itself, to snap up a bargain with intent to reauction it at their own houses at a profit. With the resident proprietor one of this gentry is about as popular as a bat in a boarding school, but since there is no law to bar him out and since it is in the line of business for him to be present, why present he generally is.

Rich women drive up in their town cars and shabby purveyors of antique wares from little clutter-hole shops on cross streets at the fringe of the East Side shamble in on their flat arches. Then, too, there are the habitués of the auction room habit; women mostly, but some men too, unfortunate creatures who have fallen victim to an incurable vice and to whom the announcement in the papers of an unusual sale is lure sufficient to draw them hither whether or not they hope to buy anything; and finally there are representatives of a common class in any big city—individuals who go wherever free entertainment is provided and especially to spots where they are likely to see assembled notables of the stage or society or of high financial circles.

The auctioneer almost invariably is of a compounded and composite type that might be described as part matinée idol, part professional revivalist, part floor walker, part court jester and part jury pleader, with just a trace of a suggestion of the official manner of the well-to-do undertaker stirred into the mixture. By sight at least he knows all of his regular customers and is inclined with a special touch of respectful affection toward such of them as prefer on these occasions to be known by an initial rather than by name.

"And sold to Mr. B.," he says with a gracious smile. Or—"Now then, Mrs. H., doesn't this bea-u-tiful varse mean anything to you?" he inquires deferentially when the bidding lags. "Did I hear you offer seven hundred and fifty, Colonel J.?" he asks in a tone of deep solicitude.

By long acquaintance with his regular clientèle, or perhaps by a sort of intuition which is not the least of his gifts, he is able to interpret into sums of currency a nod, a wink, a raised finger, a shrug or the lift of an eyebrow, at a distance of anywhere from ten to sixty feet.

In the face of disappointments manifolded a thousand times a month this man yet remains an unfailing optimist. Watching him in action one gets the impression that he reads none but glad books, goes to none save glad plays and when the weather is inclement shares the viewpoint of that sweet singer of the Sunny South who wrote to the effect that it is not raining rain to-day, it's raining daffodils, and then two lines further along corrects his botany to state that having been convinced of his error of a moment before he now wishes to take advantage of this opportunity to inform the public that it is not raining rain to-day, but on the contrary is raining roses down, or metrical words to that general tenor. He was a good poet, as poets go, but not the sort of person you would care to loan your best umbrella to.

In another noticeable regard our auctioneer friend betrays somewhat the same abrupt shiftings of temperamental manifestations that are reputed to have been shown by Ben Bolt's lady friend. I am speaking of the late lamented Sweet Alice, who—as will be recalled—

would weep with delight when you gave her a smile, but trembled with fear at your frown. Apparently Alice couldn't help behaving in this curious way—one gathers that she must have been the village idiot, harmless enough but undoubtedly an annoying sort of person to have hanging round, weeping copiously whenever anybody else was cheerful, and perhaps immediately afterward trembling in a disconcerting sort of way. She must have spoiled many a pleasant party in her day, so probably it was just as well that the community saw fit to file her away in the old churchyard in the obscure corner mentioned more or less rhythmically in the disclosures recorded as having been made to Mr. Bolt upon the occasion of his return to his native shire after what presumably had been a considerable absence.

The poet chronicler, Mr. English, is a trifle vague on this point, but considering everything it is but fair to infer that Alice's funeral was practically by acclamation. Beyond question it must have been a relief to all concerned, including the family of deceased, to feel that a person so grievously afflicted mentally was at last permanently planted under a certain slab of stone rather loosely described in the conversation just referred to as granite so gray. One wishes Mr. English had been a trifle more exact in furnishing the particular details of this sad case. Still, I suppose it is hard for a poet to be technical and poetical at the same time. And though he failed to go into particulars I am quite sure that when asked if he didn't remember Alice, Mr. Bolt answered in the decided affirmative. It is a cinch he couldn't have forgotten her, the official half-wit and lightning-change artist of the county.

But whereas this unfortunate young woman's conduct may only be accounted for on the grounds of a total irresponsibility, there is method behind the same sharply contrasted shift of mood as displayed by the chief salesman of the auction room. He is thrilled—visibly and physically thrilled—at each rapidly recurring opportunity of presenting an article for disposal to the highest bidder; hardly can he control his emotions of joy at the prospect of offering this particular object to an audience of discriminating tastes and balanced judgment. But mark the change: How instantly, how completely does a devastating and poignant distress overcome him when his hearers perversely decline to enter into spirited competition for a thing so priceless! A sob rises in his throat, choking his utterance to a degree where it becomes impossible for him to speak more than three or four hundred words per minute; grief dims his eye; regret—not on his own account but for others—droops his shoulders. When it comes to showing distress he makes that poor feeble-minded Alice girl look like a beginner. Yet repeated shocks of this character fail to daunt the sunniness of his true nature. The harder his spirits are dashed down to earth the greater the resiliency and the buoyancy with which they bounce up again. The man has a soul of new rubber!

Let us draw near and scrutinize the scene that unfolds itself at each presentation: The attendants fetch out an offering described in the printed catalogue, let us say, as Number 77 A: Oriental Lamp with Silk Shade. Reverently they place it upon a velvet-covered stand in a space at the back end of the salesroom, where a platform is inclosed in draperies with lights so disposed overhead and in the wings as to shed a soft radiance upon the inclosed area. The helpers fade out of the picture respectfully. A tiny pause ensues; this stage wait has been skillfully timed; a suitable atmosphere subtly has been created. Oh, believe me, in New York we do these things with a proper regard for the dramatic values—culture governs all!

The withdrawal of the attendants is the cue for our sunny friend, perched up as he is behind his little pulpit with his little gavel in his hand, to fall gracefully into a posture bespeaking in every curve of it a worshipful, almost an idolatrous admiration.

"And now, ladies and gentlemen"—hear him say it—"I have the pleasure and the privilege of submitting for your approval one of the absolute gems of this splendid collection. A magnificent example of the Ming period—mind you, a genuine Ming. I am confidentially informed by the executors of the estate of the late Mr. Gezinks, the former owner of these wonderful belongings, that it was the prize piece of his entire collection. Look at the color—just look at the shape! Worth a thousand dollars if it is worth a cent. Try to buy it in one of the antique shops round the corner for that—just try, that's all I ask you to do. Now then"—this with a cheery, inviting, confident smile—"now then, what am I offered? Who'll start it off at five hundred?"

There is no answer. A look of surprise not unmixed with chagrin crosses his mobile countenance. From his play of expression you feel that what he feels, underlying his other feelings, is a sympathy for people so blinded to their own good luck as not to leap headlong and en masse at this unparalleled chance.

"Tut tut!" he exclaims and again, "tut tut! Very well, then,"—his tone is resigned—"do I hear four hundred and seventy-five—four hundred and fifty? Who'll start it at four twenty-five?"

His gaze sweeps the faces of the assemblage. It is a compelling gaze, indeed you might say mesmeristic. There is a touch of pathos in it, though, an unuttered appeal to the gathering to consider its own several interests.

"Do I hear four hundred?" He speaks of four hundred as an ostrich might speak of a tomtit's egg—as something comparatively insignificant and puny.

"Twenty dollars!" pipes a voice.

He clasps his hand to his brow. This is too much; it is much too much. But business is business. He rallies; he smiles bitterly, wanly. His soul within him is crushed and bruised, but he rallies. Rallying is one of the best things he does and one of the most frequent. The bidding livens, slackens, lags, then finally ceases. With a gesture betokening utter despair, with lineaments bathed in the very waters of woe, he heart-brokenly knocks the vase down to somebody for $38.50.

But by the time the hired men have fetched forth Lot 78 he miraculously has recovered his former confidence and for the forty-oddth time since two o'clock—it is now nearly three forty-five—is his old cheerful beaming self. Thirty seconds later his heart has been broken in a fresh place; yet we may be sure that to-morrow morning when he rises he will be whistling a merry roundelay, his faith in the innate goodness of human nature all made new and fully restored to him. He would make a perfectly bully selection if you were sending a messenger to a home to break to an unsuspecting household some such tragic tidings, say; as that the head of the family, while rounding a turn on high, had skidded and was now being removed from the front elevation of an adjacent brick wall with a putty knife. If example counted for anything at all, he would have the mourners all cheered up again and the females among them discussing the most becoming modes in black crêpe in less than no time at all.

My, my, but how my sense of understanding did broaden under the influence of the auction sales we attended through the spring and on into the summer. When the morning paper came we would turn to the advertising section and look for auction announcements. If there was to be one, and generally there was—one or more—we canceled all other plans and attended. Going to auctions became our regular employment, our pastime, our entertainment. It became our obsession. It almost became our joint calling in life. To our besetting mania we sacrificed all else.

I remember there was one afternoon when John McCormack was billed to sing. I am very fond of hearing John McCormack. For one thing, he generally sings in a language which I can understand, and for another, I like his way of singing. He sings very much as I would sing if I had decided to take up singing for a living instead of writing. This is only one of the sacrifices I have made for the sake of English literature.

McCormack that day had to struggle through without me. Because there was a sale of Italian antiques billed for three P.M., and we were going to have an Italian hall and an Italian living room in the new house, and we felt it to be our bounden duty to attend.

It took some time and considerable work on the part of those fitted to guide me in the matter of decorations before I fell entirely into the idea of an Italian room, this possibly being due to the fact that I was born so far away from Italy and passed through childhood with so few Italian influences coming into my life. Even now I balk at the idea of hanging any faded red-silk stoles or copes, or whatever those ecclesiastical garments are, on my walls. I reserve the right to admire such a vestment when it is worn by the officiating cleric at church, but for the life of me and despite all that has repeatedly been said to me on the subject I fail to see where it belongs in a simple household as a part of the scheme of ornamentation.

I do not think it proper to display a strange clergyman's cast-off costume in my little home any more than I would expect the canon of a cathedral to let me hang up a pair of my old overalls in his cathedral. Nor—if I must confess it—have I felt myself greatly drawn to the suggestion that we should have a lot of tall hand-painted candles sitting or standing round in odd spots. I mean those candlesticks which are painted in faded colors, with touches of dull gilt here and there on them and which are called after a lady named Polly Crome—their original inventor, I suppose she was, though her name does sound more as if Arnold Bennett had written her than as if she were a native Italian. I imagine she thought up this idea of a hand-painted candlestick nine feet tall and eighteen inches through at the base, and then in her honor the design was called after her, which in my humble opinion was compounding one mistake on top of another.

Likewise I fear that I shall never become entirely reconciled to these old-model Italian chairs. My notion of a chair is something on which a body can sit for as long as half an hour without anesthetics. In most other details concerning antique furniture they have made a true believer out of me, but as regards chairs I am still some distance from being thoroughly converted. In chairs I favor a chair that is willing to meet you halfway, as it were, in an effort to be mutually comfortable. The other kind—the kind with a hard flat wooden seat and short legs and a stiff high back, a chair which looks as though originally it had been designed to be used by a clown dog in a trained animal act—may be artistic and beautiful in the chasteness of its lines and all this and that; but as for me, I say give me the kind of chair that has fewer admirers and more friends in the fireside circle. I take it that the early Italians were not a sedentary race. They could not have figured on staying long in one place.

I suppose the trouble with me is that I was born and brought up on the American plan and have never entirely got over it. In fact I was told as much, though not perhaps in exactly those words, when antiques first became a vital issue in our domestic life. In no uncertain terms I was informed that everybody who is anybody goes in for the Italian these times. I believe the only conspicuous exceptions to the rule are the Italians who have emigrated to these shores. They, it would appear, are amply satisfied with American fixtures and fittings. I have a suspicion that possibly some of them in coming hither may have been actuated by a desire to get as far away as possible from those medieval effects in plumbing which seem to be inseparable from Old World architecture.

My education progressed another step forward on the occasion of my first visit to an auction room where presumably desirable pieces of Italian workmanship were displayed as a preliminary to their being disposed of by public outcry. I was accompanied by a friend—the wormholeist already mentioned—and when he lapsed into rhapsodies over a pair of gilt mirrors, or rather mirrors which once upon a time, say about the time of the Fall of the Roman Empire, had been gilded, I was astonished.

"Surely," I said, "nobody would want those things. See where the glass is flawed—the quicksilver must be pretty nearly all gone from the backs of them. And the molding is falling off in chunks and what molding is left is so dingy and stained that it doesn't look like anything at all. If you're asking me, I'd call those mirrors a couple of total losses."

"Exactly!" he said. "That is precisely what makes them so desirable. You can't counterfeit such age as these things show, my boy."

"I shouldn't care to try," I said. "Where I came from, when a mirror got in such shape that you couldn't see yourself in it it was just the same to us as a chorus girl that had both legs cut off in a railroad accident—it was regarded as having lost most of its practical use in life. Still, it is not for me, a raw green novice, a sub-novice as you might say, to set myself up against an expert like you. Anyhow, as the fellow said, live and learn. Let us move along to the next display of moldy remains."

We did so. We came to a refectory table. Ordinarily a refectory table mainly differs in outline from the ordinary dining table by being constructed on the model of a dachshund. But this table, I should guess offhand, had seen about four centuries of good hard steady refecting at the hands of succeeding generations of careless but earnest feeders. Its top was chipped and marred by a million scars, more or less. Its legs were scored and worn down. Its seams gaped. From sheer weakness it canted far down to one side. The pressure of a hand upon it set the poor, slanted, crippled wreck to shaking as though along with all its other infirmities it had a touch of buck ague.

"What about this incurable invalid?" I asked. "Unless the fellow who buys it sends it up in a padded ambulance it'll be hard to get it home all in one piece. I suppose that makes it all the more valuable, eh?"

"Absolutely!" he said. "It's a perfectly marvelous thing! I figure it should bring at least six hundred dollars."

"And cheap enough," I said. "Why, it must have at least six hundred dollars' worth of things the matter with it. A good cabinet-maker could put in a nice busy month just patching—"

"You don't understand," he said. "You surely wouldn't touch it?"

"I shouldn't dare to," I said. "I was speaking of a regular cabinet-maker. No green hand should touch it—he'd have it all in chunks in no time."

"But the main value of it lies in leaving it in its present shape," he told me. "Don't you realize that this is a condition which could never be duplicated by a workman?"

"Well, I've seen some house wreckers in my time who could produce a pretty fair imitation," I retorted playfully. I continued in a musing vein, for the sight of that hopelessly damaged wreck all worn down and dented in and slivered off had sent my mind backward to a memory of early childhood. I said:

"I can see now how my parents made a mistake in stopping me from doing something I tackled when I was not more than six years old. I was an antiquer, but I didn't know it and they didn't know it. They thought that I was damaging the furniture, when as a matter of fact in my happy, innocent, childish way I was adding touches to it which would have been worth considerable money by now."

What I was thinking of was this: On my sixth birthday, I think it was, an uncle of mine for whom I was named gave me a toy tool chest containing a complete outfit of tools. There was a miniature hammer and a plane and a set of wooden vises and a gimlet and the rest of the things which belong in a carpenter's kit, but the prize of the entire collection to my way of thinking was a cross-cut saw measuring about eight inches from tip to tip.

Armed with this saw, I went round sawing things, or rather trying to. I could not exactly saw with it, but I could haggle the edges and corners of wood, producing a gnawed, frazzled effect. My quest for stuff suitable to exercise my handicraft on led me into the spare, or company room, where I found material to my liking. I was raking away at the legs of a rosewood center table—had one leg pretty well damaged to my liking and was preparing to start on another—when some officious grown person happened in on me and stopped me with violent words. If I had but been left undisturbed for half an hour or so I doubtless would have achieved a result which now after a lapse of thirty-odd years would have thrilled a lover of antiques to the core of his being. But this was not to be.

My present recollection of the incident is that I was chided in a painful physical way. The latter-day system of inculcating lessons in the mind of the child according to a printed form chart of soothing words was not known in our community at that time. The old-fashioned method of using the back of a hairbrush and imparting the lesson at the other end of the child from where the mind is and letting it travel all the way through him was employed. I was then ordered to go outdoors where there would be fewer opportunities for engaging in what adults mistakenly called mischief.

Regretting that the nurse that morning had seen fit to encase me in snug-fitting linen breeches instead of woolen ones, I wandered about carrying my saw in one hand and with the other hand from time to time rubbing a certain well-defined area of my small person to allay the afterglow.

In the barnyard I came upon an egg lying on the edge of a mud puddle under the protecting lee of the chicken-yard fence. I can shut my eyes and see that egg right now. It was rather an abandoned-looking egg, stained and blotched with brownish-yellow spots. It had the look about it of an egg with a past—a fallen egg, as you might say.

Some impulse moved me to squat down and draw the toothed blade of my saw thwartwise across the bulge of that egg. For the first time in my little life I was about to have dealings with a genuine antique, but naturally at my age and with my limited experience I did not realize that. Probably I was actuated only by a desire to find out whether I could saw right through the shell of an egg amidships. That phase of the proceedings is somewhat blurred in my mind, though the dénouement remains a vivid memory spot to this very day.

I imparted a brisk raking movement to the saw. It is my distinct recollection that a fairly loud explosion immediately occurred. I was greatly shocked. One too young to know aught of the chemical effect on the reactions following the admission of fresh air to gaseous matter, which has been forming to the fulminating point within a tightly sealed casing, would naturally be shocked to have an egg go off suddenly in that violent manner. Modern military science, I suppose, would classify it as having been a contact egg.

Not only was I badly shocked, but also I had a profound conviction that in some way I had been taken advantage of—that my confidence had in some strange fashion been betrayed. I left my saw where I had dropped it. At the moment I felt that never again would I care to have anything to do with a tool so dangerous. I also left the immediate vicinity of where the accident had occurred and for some minutes wandered about in rather a distracted fashion. There did not seem to be any place in particular for me to go, and yet I could not bear to stay wherever I was. I wished, as it were, to get entirely away from myself—a morbid fancy perhaps for a mere six-year-old to be having, and yet, I think, a natural one under the circumstances.

I had a conviction that I would not be welcomed indoors and at the same time realized that even out in the great open where I could get air—and air was what I especially craved—I was likely to be shunned by such persons as I might accidentally encounter. Indeed I rather shunned myself, if you get what I mean. I was filled with a general shunning sensation. I felt mortified, too. And this emotion, I found a few minutes later, was shared by the black cook, who, issuing from the kitchen door, happened upon me in the act of endeavoring to freshen up myself somewhat from a barrel of rain water which stood under the eaves. She evidently decided offhand that not only had mortification set in but that it had reached an advanced stage. Her language so indicated.

And now, after more than three and a half decades, here on Fifth Avenue more than a thousand miles remote from those infantile scenes, I was gleaning another memorable lesson about antiques. I was learning that junk ceases to be junk if only it costs enough money, and thereafter becomes treasure.

Having had this great principal fact firmly implanted in my consciousness, I shortly thereafter embarked in congenial company upon the auction-room life upon which already I have touched. We went to sales when we had anything to buy and when we had nothing to buy—somehow we did not seem to be able to stay away. The joy of bidding a thing up and maybe of having it knocked down to us undermined our pooled will power; it weakened our joint resistance.

"And sold to—" became our slogan, our shibboleth and our most familiar sentence. By day we heard it, by night it dinned in our ears as we slept, dreaming dreams of going bankrupt in this mad, delirious pursuit which had mastered us and spending our last days in a poorhouse entirely furnished in Italian antiques.

But taking everything into consideration, I must say the game was worth the candle. By degrees we acquired the furnishings for our two Italian rooms and our other rooms—which, thank heaven, are not Italian but what you might call fancy-mixed! And by degrees likewise I perfected my artistic education. Of course we made mistakes in selection, as who does not? We have a few auction-room skeletons tucked away in our closet, or to speak more exactly, in the attic of the new house. But in the main we are satisfied with what we have done and no doubt will continue to be until Italian-style furniture goes out and Aztec Indian or Peruvian Inca or Thibetan Grand Llama or some other style comes in.

And when our friends drop in for an evening we talk decorations and furnishings—it is a subject which never wears out. Mostly the women callers favor discussions of tapestries and brocades with intervals spent in fits of mutual wonder over the terrible taste shown by some other woman—not present—in buying the stuff for her house; and the men are likely to be interested in carvings or paintings; but my strong suit is wormholing in all its branches—that and patina. I am very strong on the latter subject, also. In fact among friends I am now getting to be known as the Patina Kid.

VIII

The Adventure of Lady Maude

I have dealt at length with our adventures at Fifth Avenue auction houses when we were amassing the furnishings for our Italian rooms and our Italian hallway. But I forgot to make mention of the many friends we encountered at the salesrooms—people who always before had seemed to us entirely normal, but now were plainly to be recognized for devotees of the same passion for bidding-in which had lain its insidious clutches upon us. I recall one victim in particular, a young woman whom I shall call Maude because that happens to be her name.

Chapter VIII

Theretofore this Maude lady had impressed me as being one of the sanest, most competent females of my entire acquaintance—good-looking, witty and with a fine sense of proportion. Yet behold, here she was, balanced on the edge of a folding chair in an overheated, overcrowded room, her eyes feverish with a fanatical light, a printed catalogue clutched in her left hand and her right ready to go up in signal to the hypnotic gentleman on the auctioneer's block. At a glance we knew the symptoms because in them we saw duplicated our own. We knew exactly what ailed her: She was bidding on various articles, not because she particularly wanted them, but because she feared unless she bought them some stranger might.

After the sale had ended and her excitement—and ours—had abated we exchanged confidences touching on our besetting mania.

"Just coming and buying something that I wish afterward I hadn't bought isn't the worst of it," she owned. "That is destructive only to my spending allowance. My chief trouble is that I've gotten so I can't bear to think of spending my afternoons anywhere except at this place or one of the places like it. And if there happen to be two sales going the same day at different shops I'm perfectly miserable. All the time I'm sitting in one I'm distracted by the thought that possibly I'm missing some perfectly wonderful bargain at the other. Sometimes I suspect that my intellect is beginning to give way under the strain, and then again I'm sure I'm on the verge of a nervous breakdown. My husband has his own diagnosis. He says I'm just plain nutty, as he vulgarly expresses it. He has taken to calling me Nutchita, which he says is Spanish for a little nut. You know since Scott came back from South America he just adores to show off the Spanish he learned. He loves to tell how he went to a bull fight down there and saw the gallant mandatory stab the charging parabola to the heart with his shining bolero or whatever you call it.

"He says there is no hope of curing me and he appreciates the fact that teams of horses couldn't drag me away from these auction rooms, but he suggested that maybe we might be saved from spending our last days at the almshouse if before I started out on my mad career each afternoon I'd get somebody to muffle me and tie my arms fast so I couldn't bid on anything. But even if I couldn't speak or gesticulate I could still nod, so I suppose that wouldn't help. Besides, as I said to him, I would probably attract a good deal of attention riding down Fifth Avenue with my hands tied behind my back and a gag in my mouth. But he says he'd much rather I were made conspicuous now than that I should be even more conspicuous later on at a feeble-minded institute; he says they'd probably keep me in a strait-jacket anyhow after I reached the violent stage and that I might as well begin getting used to the feeling now.

"All joking aside, though, I really did have a frightful experience last winter," she continued. "There was a sale of desirable household effects advertised to take place up at Blank's on West Forty-fifth Street and of course I went. I've spent so much of my time at Blank's these last few months I suppose people are beginning to think I live there. Well, anyway, I was one of the first arrivals and just as I got settled the auctioneer put up a basket; a huge, flat, curious-looking, wickerwork affair, it was. You never in all your life saw such a basket! It was too big for a soiled-clothes hamper and besides wasn't the right shape. And it was too flat to store things in and it didn't have any top on it either. I suppose you would just call it a kind of a basket.

"Well, the man put it up and asked for bids on it, but nobody bid; and then the auctioneer looked right at me in an appealing sort of way—I feel that everybody connected with the shop is an old friend of mine by now, and especially the auctioneer—so when he looked in my direction with that yearning expression in his eye I bid a dollar just to start it off for him. And what do you think? Before you could say scat he'd knocked it down to me for a dollar. I just hate people who catch you up suddenly that way! It discouraged me so that after that the sale was practically spoiled for me. I didn't have the courage to bid on another thing the whole afternoon.

"When the sale was over I went back to the packing room to get a good look at what I'd bought. And, my dear, what do you suppose? I hadn't bought a single basket—that would have been bad enough—but no. I'd bought a job lot, comprising the original basket and its twin sister that was exactly like it, only homelier if anything, and on top of that an enormous square wooden box painted a bright green with a great lock fastening the lid down. That wretch of an auctioneer had deliberately taken a shameful advantage of me. How was I to know I was bidding in a whole wagonload of trash? Obtaining money under false pretenses, that's what I call it.

"Well, I stood aghast—or perhaps I should say I leaned aghast, because the shock was so great I felt I had to prop myself up against something. Why, the box alone must have weighed a hundred and fifty pounds. It didn't seem to be the sort of box you could put anything in either. It wouldn't do for a wood box or a coal box or a dog house or anything. It was just as useless as the baskets were, and they were nothing more nor less than two orders of willow-ware on the half shell. Even if they had been of any earthly use, what could I do with them in the tiny three-room apartment that we were occupying last winter? Isn't it perfectly shameful the way these auction-room people impose on the public? They don't make any exceptions either. Here was I, a regular customer, and just see what they had done to me, all because I'm so good-natured and sympathetic. I declare sometimes I'm ready to take a solemn oath I'll never do another favor for anybody so long as I live. It's the selfish ones who get along in this world!

"Well, when I realized what a scandalous trick had been played on me I was seized with a wild desire to get away. I decided I would try to slip out. But the manager had his eye on me. You know the rule they have: 'Claim all purchases and arrange for their removal before leaving premises, otherwise goods will be stored at owner's risk and cost.' And he called me back and told me my belongings were ready to be taken away and would I kindly get them out of the house at once because they took up so much room. Room? They took up all the room there was. You had to step into one of the baskets to get into the place and climb over the box to get out again.

"I asked him how I was going to get those things up to my address and he suggested a taxi. I told him I would just run out and find a taxi, meaning, of course, to forget to come back. But he told me not to bother because there was a taxi at the door that had been ordered to come for somebody else and then wasn't needed. And before I could think up any other excuse to escape he'd called the taxi driver in. And the taxi man took one look at my collection of junk and then he asked us if we thought he was driving a moving van or a Noah's ark and laughed in a low-bred way and went out.

"At that I had a faint ray of hope that maybe after all I might be saved, because I had made up my mind to tell the manager I would just step outside and arrange to hire a delivery wagon or something, and that would give me a chance to escape; but I think he must have suspected something from my manner because already he was calling in another taxi driver from off the street, and there I was, trapped. And the driver of the second taxi was more accommodating than the other one had been, though goodness knows his goodness of heart was no treat to me. I should have regarded it as a personal kindness on his part if he had behaved as the first driver had done. But no, nothing would do but that he must load that ghastly monstrosity of a box up alongside him on the rack where they carry trunks, and two of the packing-room men tied it on with ropes so it couldn't fall off and get lost. I suppose they thought by that they were doing me a favor! And then I got in the cab feeling like Marie Antoinette on her way to be beheaded, and they piled those two baskets in on top of me and the end of one of them stuck out so far that they couldn't get the door shut but had to leave it open. And then we rode home, only I didn't feel like Marie Antoinette any more; I felt like something that was being delivered in a crate and had come partly undone on the way.

"And when we got up to Eighty-ninth Street that bare-faced robber of a taxicab driver charged me two extra fares—just think of such things being permitted to go on in a city where the police are supposed to protect people! And then he unloaded all that mess on the sidewalk in front of the apartment house and drove off and left me there standing guard over it—probably the forlornest, most helpless object in all New York at that moment.

"I got one of the hallboys to call the janitor up from the basement and I asked him if he would be good enough to store my box and my two baskets in the storeroom where the tenants keep their trunks. And he said not on my life he wouldn't, because there wasn't any room to spare in the trunk room and then he asked me what I was going to do with all that truck anyway, and though it was none of his business I thought it would be tactful to make a polite answer and I told him I hadn't exactly decided yet and that I certainly would appreciate his kindness if he could just tuck my things away in some odd corner somewhere until I had fully made up my mind. While I was saying that I was giving him one of my most winning smiles, though it hurt like the toothache to smile under the circumstances and considering what I'd already been through.

"But all he said was: 'Huh, lady, you couldn't tuck them things away at Times Square and Forty-third Street and that's the biggest corner I knows of in this town.'

"The impudent scoundrel wouldn't relent a mite either, until I'd given him a dollar for a tip, and then he did agree to keep the baskets in the coal cellar for a couple of days but no longer. But he absolutely refused to take the box along too, so I had to have it sent upstairs to the apartment and put in the bedroom because it was too big to go in the hall. And when the men got it in the bedroom I could hardly get in myself to take off my hat. And after that I sat down and cried a little, because really I was frightfully upset, and moreover I had a feeling that when Scott came home he would be sure to try to be funny. You know how husbands are, being one yourself!

"Sure enough, when he came in the first thing he saw was that box. He couldn't very well help seeing it because he practically fell over it as he stepped in the door. He said: 'What's this?' and I said: 'It's a box'—just like that. And he said: 'What kind of a box?' And I didn't like his tone and I said: 'A green box. I should think anybody would know that much.' And he said: 'Ah, indeed,' several times in a most aggravating way and walked round it. He couldn't walk all the way round it on account of the wall being in the way; but as far round it as he could walk without bumping into the wall. And he looked at it and felt it with his hand and kicked it once or twice and then he sniffed and said: 'And what's it for?' And I said: 'To put things in.' And he said: 'For instance, what?'

"Now I despise for people to be so technical round me, and besides, of all the words in the English language I most abhor those words 'for instance'; but I kept my temper even if I was boiling inside and I said: 'It's to put things in that you haven't any other place to put them in.' Which was ungrammatical, I admit, but the best I could do under the prevalent conditions. And then he looked at me until I could have screamed, and he said: 'Maude, where did you get that damned thing?' And I said it wasn't a damned thing but a perfectly good box made out of wood and painted green and everything; and that I'd got it at an auction sale for a dollar and that I considered it a real bargain. I didn't feel called on to tell him about the two baskets down in the coal cellar just yet. So I didn't mention them; and anyhow, heaven knows I was sick and tired of the whole subject and ready to drop it, but he kept on looking at it and sniffing and asking questions. Some people have no idea how a great strong brute of a man can nag a weak defenseless woman to desperation when he deliberately sets out to do it.

"Finally I said: 'Well, even if you don't like the box I think it's a perfectly splendid box, and look what a good strong lock it has on it—surely that's worth something.' And he said: 'Well, let's see about that—where's the key?' And, my dear, then it dawned on me that I didn't have any key!

"Well, a person can stand just so much and no more. I'm a patient long-suffering woman and I've always been told that I had a wonderful disposition, but there are limits. And when he burst out laughing and wouldn't stop laughing but kept right on and laughed and laughed and leaned up against something and laughed some more until you could have heard him in the next block—why then, all of a sudden something seemed to give way inside of me and I burst out crying—I couldn't hold in another second—and I told him that I'd never speak to him again the longest day he lived and that he could go to Halifax or some other place beginning with the same initial and take the old box with him for all I cared; and just as I burst out of the room I

The Adventure of Lady Maude

heard him say: 'No, madam, when I married you I agreed to support you, but I didn't engage to take care of any air-tight, burglar-proof, pea-green box the size of a circus cage!' And I suppose he thought that was being funny, too. A perverted sense of humor is an awful cross to bear—in a husband!

"So I went and lay down on the living-room couch with a raging, splitting, sick headache and I didn't care whether I lived or died, but on the whole rather preferred dying. After a little he came in, trying to hold his face straight, and begged my pardon. And I told him I would forgive him if he would do just two things. And he asked me what those two things were and I told him one was to quit snickering like an idiot every few moments and the other was never to mention boxes to me again as long as he lived. And he promised on his solemn word of honor he wouldn't, but he said I must bear with him if he smiled a little bit once in a while as the evening wore on, because when he did that he would be thinking about something very funny that had happened at the office that day and not thinking about what I would probably think he was thinking about at all. And then he said how about running down to the Plaza for a nice little dinner and I said yes, and after dinner I felt braced up and strong enough to break the news to him about the two baskets.

"And he didn't laugh; in justice to him I must say that much for him. He didn't laugh. Only he choked or something, and had a very severe coughing spell. And then we went home and while he was undressing he fell over the box and barked his shins on it, and though it must have been a strain on him he behaved like a gentleman and swore only a little.

"But, my dear, the worst was yet to come! The next day I had to arrange to send the whole lot to storage because we simply couldn't go on living with that box in the only bedroom we had; and the bill for cartage came to two dollars and a quarter. After I had seen them off to the storage warehouse I tried to forget all about them. As a matter of fact they never crossed my mind again until we moved out to the country in April and then I suddenly remembered about them—getting a bill for three months' storage at two dollars a month may have had something to do with bringing them forcibly to my memory—and I telephoned in and asked the manager of the storage warehouse if he please wouldn't give them to somebody and he said he didn't know anybody who would have all that junk as a gift. So it seemed to me the best thing and the most economical thing to do would be to pay the bill to date and bring them on out to the place.

"But, as it turned out, that was a financial mistake, too. Because what with sending the truck all the way into town, thirty-eight miles and back again, and the wear and tear on the tires and the gasoline and the man's time who drove the truck and what Scott calls the overhead—though I don't see what he means by that because it is an open truck without any top to it at all—we figure, or rather Scott does, that the cost of getting them out to the country came to fourteen dollars.

"And we still have them, and if you should happen to know of anybody or should meet anybody who'd like to have two very large roomy wicker baskets and a very well-made wooden box painted in all-over design in a very good shade of green and which may contain something valuable, because I haven't been able to open it yet to find out what's inside, and with a lock that goes with it, I wish you'd tell them that they can send up to our place and get them any time that is convenient to them. Or if they don't live too far away I'd be very glad to send the things over to them. Only I'd like for them to decide as soon as possible because the gardener, who is Swedish and awfully fussy, keeps coming in every few days and complaining about them and asking why I don't have them moved out of the greenhouse, which is where we are keeping them for the present, and put some other place where they won't be forever getting in his way. Only there doesn't seem to be any other suitable place to keep them in unless we build a shed especially for that purpose. Isn't it curious that sometimes on a hundred-acre farm there should be so little spare room? I should hate to go to the added expense of building that shed, and so, as I was saying just now, if you should happen upon any one who could use those baskets and that box please don't forget to tell them about my offer."

IX

Us Landed Proprietors

To the best of my ability I have been quoting Lady Maude verbatim; but if unintentionally I have permitted any erroneous quotations to creep into her remarks they will be corrected before these lines reach the reader's eye, because the next time she and Scott come over—they are neighbors of ours out here in Westchester—I mean to ask her to read copy on this book. They drop in on us quite frequently and we talk furnishings, and Scott sits by and smokes and occasionally utters low mocking sounds under his breath, for as yet he has not been entirely won over to antiques. There are times when I fear that Scott, though a most worthy person in all other regards, is hopelessly provincial. Well, I was a trifle provincial myself before I took the cure.

Perhaps I should say that sometimes we talk furnishings with Mistress Maude, but more often we talk farming problems, with particular reference to our own successes and the failures of our friends in the same sphere of endeavor. Indeed, farming is the commonest topic of conversation in our vicinity. Because, like us, nearly all our friends in this part of the country were formerly flat dwellers and because, like us, all of them have done a lot of experimenting in the line of intensified, impractical agriculture since they moved to the country.

We seek to profit by one another's mistakes, and we do—that is, we profit by them to the extent of gloating over them. Then we go and make a few glaring mistakes on our own account, and when the word of it spreads through the neighborhood, seemingly on the wings of the wind, it is their turn to gloat. We have a regular Gloat Club with an open membership and no dues. If an amateur tiller of the soil and his wife drop in on us on a fine spring evening to announce that yesterday they had their first mess of green peas, whereas our pea vines are still in the blossoming state; or if in midsummer they come for the express purpose of informing us that they have been eating roasting ears for a week—they knowing full well that our early corn has suffered a backset—we compliment them with honeyed words, and outwardly our manner may bespeak a spirit of friendly congratulation, but in our souls all is bitterness.

After they have left one catches oneself saying to one's helpmeet: "Well, the Joneses are nice people in a good many respects. Jones would loan you the last cent he had on earth if you were in trouble and needed it, and in most regards Mrs. Jones is about as fine a little woman as you'd meet in a day's ride. But dog-gone it, I wish they didn't brag so much!" Then one of us opportunely recalls that last year their potatoes developed a slow and mysterious wasting disease resembling malignant tetter, which carried off the entire crop in its infancy, whereas we harvested a cellarful of wonderful praties free from skin blemishes of whatever sort; and warmed by that delectable recollection we cheer up a bit. And if our strawberries turn out well or our apple trees bear heavily or our cow has twin calves, both of the gentler sex, we lose no time in going about the countryside to spread the tidings, leaving in our wake saddened firesides and hearts all abrim with the concentrated essence of envy.

Practically all our little group specialize. We go in for some line that is absolutely guaranteed to be profitable until the expense becomes too great for a person of limited means any longer to bear up under. Then we drop that and specialize in another line, also recommended as being highly lucrative, for so long as we can afford it; and then we tackle something else again. It is a never-ending round of new experiences, because no matter how disastrously one's most recent experiment has turned out the agricultural weeklies are constantly holding forth the advantages of a field as yet new and untried and morally insured to be one that will yield large and nourishing dividends. It is my sober conviction that the most inspired fiction writers in America—the men with the most buoyant imaginations—are the regular contributors to our standard agricultural journals. And next to them the most gifted romancers are the fellows who sell bulbs and seeds. They are not fabulists exactly, because fables have morals and frequently these persons have none, but they are inspired fanciers, I'll tell the world.

Each succeeding season finds each family among us embarking upon some new and fascinating venture. For instance, I have one friend who this year went in for bees—Italian bees, I think he said they were, though why he should have been prejudiced against the native-born variety I cannot understand. He used to drop in at our place to borrow a little cooking soda—he was constantly running out of cooking soda at his house owing to using so much of it on his face and hands and his neck for poulticing purposes—and tell us what charming creatures bees were and how much honey he expected to lay by that fall. From what he said we gathered that the half had never been told by Maeterlinck about the engaging personal habits and captivating tribal customs of bees; bees, we gathered, were, as a race, perhaps a trifle quick-tempered and hot-headed, or if not exactly hot-headed at least hot elsewhere, but ever ready to forgive and forget and, once the heat of passion had passed, to let bygones be bygones. A bee, it seemed from his accounts, was one creature that always stood ready to meet you halfway.

He finally gave up bee culture though, not because his enthusiasm had waned, for it did not, but for professional reasons solely. He is a distinguished actor and when he got the leading rôle in a new play it broke in on his study of the part to be dropping the manuscript every few minutes and grabbing up a tin dish and running out in an endeavor, by the power of music, to induce a flock of swarming bees to rehive themselves, or whatever it is bees are supposed to do when favored with a pie-pan solo. It seemed his bees had a perfect mania for swarming. The least little thing would set them off. There must have been too much artistic temperament about the premises for such emotional and flighty creatures as bees appear to be.

Then there was another reason: After the play went on he found it interfered with his giving the best that was in him to his art if he had to go on for a performance all bumpy in spots; also he discovered that grease paint had the effect of irritating a sting rather than soothing it. The other afternoon he came over and offered to give me his last remaining hive of bees. Indeed, he almost pressed them on me.

I declined though. I told him to unload his little playmates on some stranger; that I valued his friendship and hoped to keep it; the more especially, as I now confessed to him, since I had lately thought that if literature ever petered out I might take up the drama as a congenial mode of livelihood, and in such case would naturally benefit through the good offices of a friend who was already in the business and doing well at it. Not, however, that I felt any doubt regarding my ultimate success. I do not mean by this that I have seriously considered playwriting as a regular profession. Once I did seriously consider it, but nobody else did, and especially the critics didn't. Remembering what happened to the only dramatic offering I ever wrote, I long ago made up my mind that if ever I wrote another play—which, please heaven, I shall not—I would call it Solomon Grundy, whether I had a character of that name in it or not. You may recall what happened to the original Solomon Grundy—how he was born on a Monday, began to fail on Thursday, passed away on Saturday of the same week and was laid to eternal rest on Sunday. So even though I never do another play I have the name picked out and ready and waiting.

No, my next venture into the realm of Thespis, should necessity direct my steps thither, would land me directly upon the histrionic boards. Ever since I began to fill out noticeably I have nourished this ambition secretly. As I look at it, a pleasing plumpness of outline should be no handicap but on the contrary rather a help. My sex of course is against my undertaking to play The Two Orphans, otherwise I should feel no doubt of my ability to play both of them, and if they had a little sister I shouldn't be afraid to take her on, too. But I do rather fancy myself in the title rôles of The Corsican Brothers. If I should show some enterprising manager how he might pay out one salary and save another, surely the idea would appeal to him; and some of these fine days I may give the idea a try. So having this contingency in mind I gently but firmly told my friend to take his bees elsewhere. I told him I had no intention of looking a gift bee in the mouth.

We have another neighbor who has gone in rather extensively for blooded stock with the intention ultimately of producing butter and milk for the city market. During practically all his active life he has been a successful theatrical manager, which naturally qualifies him for the cow business. He is doing very well at it too. So long as he continues to enjoy successful theatrical seasons he feels that he will be able to go on with cows. Being a shrewd and farseeing business man he has it all figured out that a minimum of three substantial enduring hits every autumn will justify him in maintaining his herd at its present proportions, whereas with four shows on Broadway all playing to capacity he might even increase it to the extent of investing in a few more head of registered thoroughbred stock.

From him I have gleaned much regarding cows. Before, the life of a cow fancier had been to me as a closed book. Generally speaking, cows, so far as my personal knowledge went, were divided roughly into regular cows running true to sex, and the other kind of cows, which were invariably referred to with a deep blush by old-fashioned maiden ladies. True enough, we owned cows during the earlier stages of our rural life; in fact, we own one now, a mild-eyed creature originally christened Buttercup but called by us Sahara because of her prevalent habits. But gentle bone-dry Sahara is just a plain ordinary cow of undistinguished ancestry. In the preceding generations of her line scandal after scandal must have occurred; were she a bagpipe solo instead of a cow scarcely could she have in her more mixed strains than she has. We acquired her at a bargain in an auction sale; she is a bargain to any one desiring a cow of settled and steady habits, regular at her meals, always with an unfailing appetite and having a deep far-reaching voice. There is also an expectation that some future day we may also derive from her milk. However, this contingency rests, as one might say, upon the laps of the gods.

The point I am getting at though is that Sahara, whatever else of merit she may possess in the matters of a kind disposition and a willingness to eat whatever is put before her, is after all but a mere common country-bred cow; whereas the cows whose society my wealthy neighbor cultivates are the pedigreed aristocrats of their breed, and for buying and selling purposes are valued accordingly. Why, from the way the proprietors of registered cows brag about their ancient lineage and their blue-blooded forbears you might think they were all from South Carolina or Massachusetts—the cows, I mean, not necessarily the proprietors.

So it is with the man of whom I have been speaking. Having become a breeder of fancy stock he now appraises a cow not for what she can do on her own intrinsic merits but for the size of her family tree, provided she brings with her the documents to prove it. So far as cows are concerned he has become a confirmed ancestor worshipper. I am sure he would rather own a quarter interest in a collateral descendant of old Prince Bullcon the First of the royal family of the Island of Guernsey, even though the present bearer of the name were but an indifferent milker and of unsettled habits, than to be the sole possessor of some untitled but versatile cow giving malted milk and whipped cream. Such vagaries I cannot fathom. In a democratic country like this, or at least in a country which used to be democratic, it seems to me we should value a cow not for what her grandparents may have been; not for the names emblazoned on her genealogical record, but for what she herself is.

The other Sunday we drove over to his place ostensibly to pay a neighborly call but really to plant distress in his fireside circle by incidentally mentioning that our young grapevines were bearing magnificently.

You see, a member of the Gloat Club is expected to work at his trade Sundays as well as weekdays; and besides we had heard that his arbors, with the coming of the autumn, had seemed a bit puny. So the opportunity was too good to be lost and we went over.

After I had driven the harpoon into his soul and watched it sink into him up to the barbs he took me out to see the latest improvements he had made in his cow barn and to call upon the newest addition to his herd. These times you can bed a hired hand down almost anywhere, but if you go in for blooded stock you must surround them with the luxuries to which they have been accustomed, else they are apt to go into a decline. He invited my inspection of the porcelain-walled stalls and the patent feeding devices and the sanitary fixtures which abounded on every hand, and to his recently installed cream separator. In my youth the only cream separator commonly in vogue was the type of drooping mustache worn by the average deputy sheriff, and anyhow, with it, cream separating was merely incidental, the real purposes of the mustache being to be ornamental and impressive and subtly to convey a proper respect for the majesty of the law. Often a town marshal wore one too. But the modern separator is a product of science and not a gift of Nature skillfully elaborated by the art of the barber. It costs a heap of money and it operates by machinery and no really stylish dairy farm is complete without it.

When I had viewed these wonders he led me to a glorified pasture lot and presented me to the occupant—a smallish cow of a prevalent henna tone. Except that she had rather slender legs and a permanent wave between the horns she seemed to my uninitiated eyes much the same as any other cow of the Jersey persuasion. I realized, however, that she must be very high-church. My friend, I knew, would harbor no nonconformist cows in his place, and besides, she distinctly had the high-church manner, a thing which is indefinable in terms of speech but unmistakably to be recognized wherever found. Otherwise, though, I could observe nothing about her calculated to excite the casual passer-by. But my friend was all enthusiasm.

"Now," he said proudly, "what do you think of that for a perfect specimen?"

"Well," I said, "anybody could tell that she's had a lot of refining influences coming into her life. She's no doubt cultured and ladylike to a degree; and she has the fashionable complexion of the hour and she's all marcelled up and everything, but excepting for these adornments has she any special accomplishments that are calculated to give her class?"

"Class!" he repeated. "Class, did you say? Say, listen! That cow has all the class there is. She's less than two years old and she cost me a cool fifteen hundred cash—and cheap at the figure, at that."

"Fifteen hundred," I murmured dazedly. "What does she give?"

"Why, she gives milk, of course," he explained. "What else would she be giving?"

"Well," I said, "I should think that at that price she should at least give music lessons. Perhaps she does plain sewing?"

"Say," he demanded, "what do you expect for fifteen hundred dollars? Fifteen hundred is a perfectly ridiculous price to pay for a cow with a pedigree such as this cow has. She's registered back I don't know how far. It's the regal breeding you pay for when you get an animal like this—not the animal herself."

But I refused to be swept off my feet. Before this I had associated with royalty. I once met a lineal descendant of William the Conqueror; he told me so himself. Being a descendant was apparently the only profession he had, and I judged this cow was in much the same line of business.

"Well," I replied, "all I can say is that I wouldn't care if her ancestors came over on the Mayflower—if she belonged to me she'd have to show me something in the line of special endeavor. She'd have to have talents or we'd part company pretty pronto, I'm telling you."

"It is evident you do not understand anything about blooded stock," he said. "The grandmother of this cow was insured for fifteen thousand dollars, and her great-grandfather, King Bulbul, was worth a fortune. The owner was offered fifty thousand for him—and refused it."

In my surprise I could only mutter over and over again the name of William Tell's brother. A great many people do not know that William Tell ever had a brother. His first name was Wat.

    After that my friend gave me up as one hopelessly sunken in ignorance, and by a mutual yet unspoken consent we turned the subject to the actors' strike, which was then in full blast. But at intervals ever since I have been thinking of what he told me. To my way of thinking there is something wrong with the economic system of a country which saddles an income tax on an unmarried man with an income of more than two thousand dollars a year and if he be married sinks the ax into all he makes above three thousand, leaving him the interest deduction on the extra one thousand, amounting, I believe, to about twelve dollars and a half, for the support of his wife, on the theory that under the present scale of living any reasonably prudent man can suitably maintain a wife on twelve-fifty a year—I repeat, there is something radically wrong with a government which does this to the wage-earner and yet passes right on by a cow that carries fifteen thousand in life insurance and a bull worth fifty thousand in his own right. It amounts to class privilege, I maintain. It's almost enough to make a man vote the Republican ticket, and I may yet do it, too, sometime when there aren't any Democrats running, just to show how I feel about it.

    Yet others of our acquaintances in the amateur-farming group have taken up fruit growing or pigeons or even Belgian hares. Belgian hares have been highly recommended to us as being very prolific. You start in with one pair of domestic-minded Belgian hares and presently countless thousands of little Belgian heirs and heiresses are gladdening the landscape. From what I can hear the average Belgian hare has almost as many aunts and uncles and cousins as a microbe has. They pay well, too. You can sell a Belgian hare to almost anybody who has never tried to eat one. But as we have only about sixty acres and part of that in woodland, we have felt that there was scarcely room enough for us to go in for Belgian hares without sacrificing space which we may require for ourselves.

Mainly our experiments have been confined to hogs and poultry. I will not claim that we have been entirely successful in these directions. The trouble seems to be that our pigs are so tremendously opposed to race suicide and that our hens are so firmly committed to it. Now offhand you might think an adult animal of the swine family that completely gave herself over to the idea of multiplying and replenishing the earth with her species would be an asset to any farm, but in my own experience I have found that such is not always the case. Into the world a brood of little pinky-white squealers are ushered. They grow apace, devouring with avidity the most expensive brands of pig food that the grocer has in stock; and then, just when your mind is filled with delectable visions of hams in the smokehouse and flitches of bacon in the cellar and tierces of lard in the cold-storage room and spare-ribs and crackling and home-made

Us Landed Proprietors

country sausage and pork tenderloins on the table—why, your prospects deliberately go and catch the hog cholera and are shortly no more. They have a perfect mania for it. They'll travel miles out of their way to catch it; they'll sit up until all hours of the night in the hope of catching it. Hogs will swim the Mississippi River—and it full of ice—to get where hog cholera is. Our hogs have been observed in the act of standing in the pen with their snouts in the air, sniffing in unison until they attracted the germs of it right out of the air. It is very disheartening to be counting on bacon worth eighty cents a pound only to find that all you have on your hands is a series of hurried interments.

In their own sphere of life turkeys are as suicidally minded as hogs are. I speak with authority here because we tried raising turkeys, too. For a young turkey to get its feet good and wet spells doom for the turkey, and accordingly it practically devotes its life to getting its feet wet. If it cannot escape from the pen into the damp grass immediately following a rain it will in its desperation take other measures with a view to catching its death of cold. One of the most distressing spectacles to be witnessed in all Nature is a half-grown feebleminded turkey obsessed with the maniacal idea that it was born a puddle duck, running round and round a coop trying to find a damp spot to stand on; it is a pitiful sight and yet exasperating. In order to get its feet wet an infant turkey has been known to jump down an artesian well two hundred feet deep. This is not mere idle rumor; it if a scientific fact well authenticated. If somebody would only invent a style of overshoe that might be worn in comfort by an adolescent turkey without making the turkey feel distraught or self-conscious, that person would confer a boon upon the entire turkey race and at the same time be in a fair way to reap a fortune for himself. I know that a few months back if such an article had been in the market I would gladly have taken fifty pairs, assorted misses' and children's sizes.

As for hens, I confess that at times I have felt like altogether abandoning my belief in the good faith and honest intentions of hens. Naturally one thinks of hens in connection with fresh-laid eggs, but my experience has been that the hen does not follow this line of reasoning. She prefers to go off on a different bent. She figures she was created to adorn society, not to gladden the breakfast platter of man. Or at any rate I would state that this has been the obsession customarily harbored by the hens which we have owned and which we persistently continue, in the face of disappointment compounded, to go on owning.

We started out by buying, at a perfectly scandalous outlay, a collection of blooded hens of the white Plymouth Rock variety. We had been told that the sun never set on a setting white Plymouth Rock hen; that a white Plymouth Rock hen which had had the right sort of influences in her life and the right sort of hereditary instincts to guide her in her maturer career would inevitably dedicate her entire being to producing eggs. And we believed it until the hens we had purchased themselves offered proof to the absolute contrary.

It was enough almost to break one's heart to see a great broad-beamed, full-busted husky hen promenading round the chicken run, eating her head off, gadding with her sister idlers, wasting the precious golden hours of daylight in idle social pursuits and at intervals saying to herself: "Lay an egg? Well, I guess not! Why should I entail a strain on my nervous system and deny myself the pleasures of the gay life for the sake of these people? If they were able to pay four dollars for me, sight unseen, they are sufficiently affluent to buy their own eggs. Am I right? I'll say I am!"

You could look at her expression and tell what she was thinking. And then when you went and made the rounds of the empty and untenanted nests you knew that you had correctly fathomed the workings of her mind.

We tried every known argument on those hens in an effort to make them see the error of their ways and the advantages of eggs. We administered to them meat scraps and fresh carrots and rutabagas and sifted gravel and ground-up oyster shells; the only result was to make them finicky and particular regarding their diet. No longer were they satisfied with the things we ate ourselves; no, they must have special dishes; they wished to be pampered like invalids. We bought for them large quantities of costly chick feed—compounds guaranteed to start the most confirmed spinster hen to laying her head off.

So far as I might observe, this, too, was of no avail. The more confirmed imbibers of the special dishes merely developed lumpy dropsical figures and sat about in shady spots and brooded in a morbid way as though they had heavy loads on their minds. We killed one of them as a sacrifice to scientific investigation and cut her open, and lo, she was burdened inside with half-developed yolks—a case, one might say, of mislaid eggs.

In desperation I even thought of invoking the power of mental suggestion on them. Possibly it might help to hang up a picture of a lady sturgeon in the henhouse? Or would it avail to shoo them into a group and read aloud to them the begat chapter in the Old Testament?

While I was considering these expedients some one suggested that probably the trouble lay in the fact that our fowls either were too highly bred or were too closely related and perhaps an infusion of new blood was what was needed. So now we went to the other extreme and added to our flock a collection of ordinary scrub hens, mixed as to breed and homely as to their outward appearance, but declared—by their former owner—to be passionately addicted to the pursuit of laying eggs. Conceding that this was true, the fact remained that immediately they passed into our possession they became slackers and nonproducers. I imagine the mistake we made was in permitting them to associate with the frivolous white débutantes we already owned; undoubtedly those confirmed bachelor maids put queer ideas into their heads, causing them to believe there was no nourishment in achieving eggs to be served up with a comparative stranger's fried ham.

On the theory that they might require exercise to stimulate their creative faculties we let them range through the meadows. Some among them promptly deserted the grassy leas to ravage our garden; others made hidden nests in the edges of the thickets, where the hawks and the weasels and the skunks and the crows might fatten on the fruits of their misdirected industry. So we cooped them up again in their run, whereupon they developed rheumatism and sore eyes and a perverted craving for eating one another's tail feathers. At present our chicken yard is nothing more nor less than a hen sanitarium. But we do not despair of ultimate success with our hens. We may have to cross them with the Potomac shad, but we mean to persevere until victory has perched upon our roosts. As Rupert Hughes remarked when, after writing a long list of plays which died a-borning, he eventually produced a riotous hit of hits: "Well, I'm only human—I couldn't fail every time."

I should have said that there is one fad to which all our Westchester County colony of amateur farmers are addicted. Some may pursue one agricultural hobby and some another, but almost without exception the members of our little community are confirmed hired-help fanciers. You meet a neighbor and he tells you that after a disastrous experience with Polled Polaks he is now about to try the White Face Cockneys; they have been highly recommended to him. And next month when you encounter him again he is experimenting with Italian road builders or Scotch gardeners or Swedish stable hands or Afro-American tree trimmers or what not.

One member of our group after a prolonged season of alternating hopes and disappointments during which he first hired and then for good and sufficient reasons fired representatives of nearly all the commoner varieties—plain and colored, domestic and imported, strays, culls and mavericks—decided to try his luck in the city at one of the employment agencies specializing in domestic servitors for country places. He procured the address of such an establishment and repaired thither—simply attired in his everyday clothes. As soon as he entered the place he realized that he was in the wrong pew; here, plainly, was a shop to which repaired the proprietors of ostentatious estates rather than the modest owners of farms, among whom he numbered himself. He tried to back out, making himself as inconspicuous as possible in so doing, but at that before he succeeded in escaping he had two good jobs offered to him—one as assistant groom in a racing stable over on Long Island and one as general handyman at a yacht club up in Connecticut. He is convinced now that the rich are so hard pressed for servants that they'll hire almost anybody without requiring references.

None of us will ever be rich; we're all convinced of that, the cost of impractical farming being what it is, but by the same token none of us would give up the pleasures of a landed proprietor's lot—the word landed being here used to imply one baited, hooked and caught; i.e., a landed sucker—for the life of a flat dweller again. It's a great life if a fellow doesn't weaken—and we'll never weaken.

The End

About the Author

Irvin Shrewsbury Cobb (1876–1944) was a journalist, fiction writer, Hollywood actor, and larger-than-life personality. Born and raised on a farm in Paducah, Kentucky, Cobb became a beloved celebrity in early twentieth-century America. Known best for his "Old Judge Priest" stories, which depicted southern local color, Cobb initially rose to fame as a combat reporter during World War I.

www.ingramcontent.com/pod-product-compliance
Lightning Source LLC
Chambersburg PA
CBHW021435080526
44588CB00009B/539